Bruising the Head of Satan

Bruising the Head of Satan

God, Jesus, and the Holy Angels Teach Mankind How to Fight Evil

Chronicled by
Farmer Mattar

Exponential Forest
www.bruisingtheheadofsatan.com
Copyright © 2012 Farmer Mattar

NOTICE OF RIGHTS

ALL RIGHTS RESERVED. No part of this book may be reproduced, stored in a retrieval system, or transmitted, in any form or by any means, electronic, mechanical, photocopying, recording, or otherwise, without the prior written permission of the publisher. Contact information is available on the website www.bruisingtheheadofsatan.com.

NOTICE OF LIABILITY

The information in this book is distributed on an "As Is" basis, without warranties of any kind, expressed or implied. While every precaution has been taken in the preparation of the book, neither the author nor the publisher shall have any liability to any person or entity with respect to any liability, loss, or damage of any kind caused or alleged to be caused directly or indirectly by the information contained in this book.

NOTICE OF PRIVACY

Some human names in this book have been altered (where requested) to protect the privacy of those involved. The author chose these names using tables of random numbers and names. Any similarity to specific individuals, living or dead, is unintentional and purely random.

See also the WARNINGS TO READERS section following the table of contents.

Published 2012
Printed in the United States of America
First Edition, First Printing (print run: 1 of the year: 2012)
∞ This edition is printed on acid-free paper that meets the requirements of ANSI/NISO Z39.48-1992 (Permanence of Paper).

ISBN: 978-0-98540-260-0 (hardcover, cloth)
ISBN: 978-0-98540-265-5 (paperback)

Contents

Warnings to Readers!   ix

Introduction

The Garden   3

Beginnings

The Farmer   9
The Mule   14
Halo of Protection   24

Luther's Game

My Name is Luther   33
The Evil Chorus   40
Light of a Different Kind   43
First Confrontation   48
Wait On the Lord and Be of Good Courage   53
The Regression   59
Pretty Angel   64
I Know All About Luther   68
Follow My Name   72
Luther Loses the Game   76

Satan's Revenge

The Days Yet to Come	85
Divine Comfort	88
The Rock	93
Angels of Distinction	100
The Baptism	106
Roaring Lion	110

Moving the Rock

The Commission	121
Rock-Moving Visions	126
The Demon of Hate	133
The Demon of Lust	139
The Evil Party	143
The Imps	149
Remember Elizabeth	156

Modus Operandi

Spiritual Paths	161
Luther's Way	164
Lustful Perversions	171
The Demon Guards	174
Katrina's Review	177

The Cherry Blossoms

The Working of the Land	181
Day of the Cherry Blossoms	187
The Farmer's Travail	194

Farmer's Conversations with Albert

Albert's Preface to the Conversations	199
Soul and Holy Spirit	200
Satan	204
Earthly Trials	208
Predestination	212
Children	215
Hell	218
The End Times	220
The Creation	223
Original Sin in the Garden of Eden	226
Male and Female	229
Demons	232
Illness and Healing	239
The Seats of Power	241
The Word of God	243
Tithes and Offerings	246
Salvation	247
Death	253
Animals	256
Chariot and Cherubim	258
Heaven	260
Holy Angels	264
Jesus	270
God the Father Almighty	276

Conclusion

I Would That All Men Would Interfere	283
So That Love Would Have Meaning	292
Albert's Word to the Oppressed	297
The Wheat Field	299
Epilogue	303

Warnings to Readers!

(The Author and Publisher Caution You to Read Them)

WARNING #1 – This book is nonfiction. The words and actions attributed to God, Jesus, holy angels, Satan, demons, and humans ARE THEIR OWN WORDS AND ACTIONS.

WARNING #2 – This book provides a detailed case history of demon possession in the life of one woman, as well as other supplementary accounts and information. This information is provided solely for the spiritual edification of the reader. The author and publisher do not purport to diagnose any disorder, nor do they recommend any specific actions be taken based on any information contained within. The reader is solely responsible for any actions they may take.

WARNING #3 – This book contains detailed accounts of some of the author's spiritual interventions against the demons so that the reader may more fully empathize with the inherent difficulties of the undertaking for both victim and intercessor. However, the reader is cautioned to NEVER DIRECTLY CONFRONT A DEMON, NOR ATTEMPT TO REPLICATE ANY OF THE DEMON-FIGHTING TECHNIQUES DESCRIBED

WITHIN. The reader will not become an expert in dealing with demons merely by reading this book. Remember, however, that nonconfrontational prayer is always appropriate and is a peaceful weapon of great power and effectiveness.

➤ A central theme of this book is the great challenge of differentiating problems that are caused by demons versus those with earthly or unknown causes. Consider:

WARNING #4 – Statistically speaking, more people have problems that are of earthly origin, rather than demonic origin.

The (approximate) incidence of demon possession of any given severity in the general U.S. population is currently 8% (33% worldwide). Half of these are severely possessed. The U.S. percentage is lower than the world percentage because of the relatively higher numbers of believers in God and Jesus in the U.S. relative to the world as a whole.

Therefore, statistically speaking, for the general U.S. population, it is usually best to rule out earthly causes to problems first because they are more probable for any given individual. Do not attempt to diagnose yourself or others. Seek the assistance of competent medical, mental health, or other expert, earthly professionals. Exhaust all earthly advice and remedies before possibly considering alternative explanations.

WARNING #5 – Should the reader ever decide to consult an expert on demonic possession or demonic influence, use extreme caution in selecting that expert. True experts are exceedingly rare. The central characteristic of all true experts on demons is a strong belief and faith in the God and Jesus of the Holy Bible, and the sole use of that belief and faith to combat the demons. Using anything else against demons would both fail and be dangerous to those involved.

WARNING #6 – This book is not intended to be an exhaustive recital of all material available to the author; it has been greatly condensed and simplified to make it more easily accessible to the reader. Always assume that many details were necessarily left out. Also, of the material that was included, the author cannot possibly clarify all possible ambiguities and dispel all possible misconceptions that might arise. Therefore, use this book only as a general guide to the subject matter and not as the sole source of information available. The reader is strongly encouraged to read the Holy Bible for a more complete understanding of the material within.

WARNING #7 – Despite the best efforts of author and publisher, this book may contain typographical, word choice, word placement, grammatical, and other editing errors that could possibly be confusing or misleading to the reader. We regret these possible errors, and would ask the reader to point them out to us if found.

NOTICE OF LIABILITY

The information in this book is distributed on an "As Is" basis, without warranties of any kind, expressed or implied. While every precaution has been taken in the preparation of the book, neither the author nor the publisher shall have any liability to any person or entity with respect to any liability, loss, or damage of any kind caused or alleged to be caused directly or indirectly by the information contained in this book.

Part I

Introduction

Because of all my love for my children and my Father, I accepted much pain without question.

— Jesus

Chapter 1

The Garden

The Lord Jesus Christ awaited the young woman's arrival in his beloved Garden of Knowledge and Contemplation within the glorious Kingdom of Heaven. The Garden was dear to Jesus, for it was here that he often communed with the distressed souls of his earthly children, though seldom would he allow them to retain the memory.

The earthly Garden of Eden had been created in the image of Heaven's Garden and for the same purpose: so that God could commune with his children. But Satan seduced, and the bond was broken. Just as Adam's and Eve's physical bodies had returned to dust, so had Eden, now nothing more than a parcel of Sudanese desert, a barren mockery of its former perfection. Yet Heaven's Garden of Knowledge and Contemplation remained as beautiful and pristine as its Maker's Spirit.

"I'm glad to see you," Jesus said as he offered his hand to the woman who now stood before him. She took Jesus' hand, and he gently escorted her down a winding cobblestone path to a backless, rough-hewn wooden bench. Jesus sat, lifted the woman onto his lap, and nestled her head against his shoulder.

And Jesus spoke: "I'm filled with pride because you turned to me and believed in me, and I helped you to get rid of Luther (not Lucifer). And you all carried out my orders so very well. I know you thought it was all over after the baptism, but you have to remember that Satan tried to tempt me three times after mine. Satan is such a jealous fool. He makes me very angry, but he never learns.

"I'm so very happy because now you've proven your love to me. Because of all my love for my children and my Father, I accepted much pain without question. You've shown me how much you love me by bearing all you have and believing I would save you. So you may not be able to say you love me, but your actions prove you do.

"I'm so pleased with all of you, and you will all get to come to the Garden someday. What a crew."

The woman said, "My head hurts."

Jesus said, "I can bet—such a headache! But you'll get better."

A passing flock of songbirds heard Jesus speaking and broke formation to claim perches in the surrounding willows. Looking upward, Jesus smiled at the birds, and they burst into song. They could not resist; they simply had to sing in Jesus' presence. As the woman well knew, Jesus made the birds sing.

The woman peeked over Jesus' shoulder and saw the familiar faces of three holy angels, sent to earth by God to help her in the fight against evil. The cherub Albert, holy angel of tidings, spoke lyrical words of knowledge; the holy guardian angel Katrina had accompanied the woman from birth; and the holy guardian angel Lucinda had always accompanied the Farmer, the woman's earthly helper. Albert, Katrina, and Lucinda smiled radiantly at the woman who sat on the lap of the One to whom they had always remained loyal.

Without so much as a glance, Jesus knew the woman had seen the angels. "I know Albert is quite a talker," Jesus said, "but at least he makes you think. Albert will still come to you, just as I will if you ask me."

Yet the battle was far from over, and Jesus encouraged the woman for the tough times ahead: "I know you love me, but I want you to love yourself and move the rock. It takes time and tears, but I've cried too."

The woman pleaded with Jesus, "Please let me stay."

Jesus said, "No, you have to go back and tell the rest of the crew what I said. The angels will be with all of you always, just as I will. Now go and tell them I love them very much."

Jesus then dispatched the essence of the woman's soul back to her earthly, physical body. She opened her eyes and smiled sweetly at the Farmer. He readied his pencil and paper to again record blessed words of the Master.

And the word of the Lord came to the woman through the cherub Albert, holy angel of tidings: "Be thee not confused of mind between that of a dream and that of an angel's prophecy: for all shall dream, while few are but chosen to be guided by quieting voices of holy angels. For those who inherit salvation as by their directions given are to share to all in hopes of uniting souls. Be assured the Lord shall allow the souls in need of belief to hear, just as ye trust in the fact he performs miraculous deeds for to deliver salvation.

"Be it known that there be multitudes of ways to tell of the Word: for many a wondering soul there are, and thus many a way to reach their hearts and touch them with the Holy Spirit be necessary. Fear not to go forth with ye endeavors: for when standing on the fertile land of the Lord, many a wind may blow, but the tree, as in the words, will live on to old age."

But the Farmer was troubled, for how was it possible to tell of all the wondrous experiences and knowledge that had been given them?

And Albert spoke: "When a man has an apple in his eye, yet sees a cherry he admires, it matters not the importance of the size or flavor. But since he may not have both, be it best to sacrifice the apple and choose in favor of the fruit with the most spiritual substance, for it is assured from Above that it will last forever.

"And though he may miss the juice of the apple, the sweetness of the cherry shall be of such magnitude, he would yearn not. For though the cherry may have a pit, the fruit surrounding it be priceless. And there be no other thing of more value than bonds of salvation and unity leading into the Land of the Fadeless Day, with constant guidance of gentle voices. Therefore, I say unto ye: discard the apple and choose the cherry, for the most blessed of value be in that of the cherry.

"When the Farmer brings his fruits to market, he shall return home with that of an empty cart. Many shall inquire of the Farmer the secrets of his hearty thumb, and he may stand proud in the profession of his faith. Yet when strolling along a valley of the greenest trees and grasses, 'tis best to enjoy that of the peacefulness; and remember: ye need not provide an endless commentary, for those who follow shall know."

Part II

Beginnings

Today is born a man who will confound the plans of the wicked. He will bruise the head of Satan.

– God the Father Almighty

Chapter 2

The Farmer

On the Nazareth parallel, God the Father proclaimed: "Today is born a man who will confound the plans of the wicked. He will bruise the head of Satan. He will do the will of my Anointed and bring honor and glory to my Name."

The female guardian angels were aflutter at the news and chattered the baby awake. Cherub Albert spoke: "Sotto voce, sisters, pray let him sleep. God calls him 'Farmer,' for he be the farmer of men's souls. Be it a name that is known in many realms, for 'tis not a secret that can be kept."

A powerful force beseeched me to come outdoors into the warm Texas night. I strapped my toy holster with six-guns around my waist and propelled my five-year-old body out the door, seating myself on the patch of grass offering the best view of the night sky.

A multitude of stars called out to me, but only one chose me. Its light was more radiant than the other stars; its pulsing, more hypnotic. The star and I simply stared at each other. As time passed and the visual bond grew more intense, a warm honey-glow filled me to overflowing.

Most amazingly, the star declared: "You know who I am."

Indeed, I did. I jumped to my feet and started bouncing up and down. "Jesus, Jesus, Jesus!" I shouted out.

Jesus laughed.

I felt like I could fly. "Watch this, Jesus!" I called up towards the star. I then spread my arms like airplane wings and ran figure eights around the yard in such a way that Jesus most certainly had to be impressed.

Jesus laughed again and gave me time to dissipate some energy.

Jesus then said, "Watch this, Farmer."

I said, "You're teasing me."

"Friends tease friends," Jesus said, "but there is something I want to show you."

Thwack. In the flash of an instant, I saw a Divine gestalt of the world's folly: Some very strange people were talking amongst themselves, saying that God did not exist, or he was an animal, or a woman, or had some funny name. Others were saying that Jesus was a myth, or he wasn't the Son of God, or he hadn't died on the cross, or he was no longer relevant. And perhaps saddest of all, some people simply didn't care one way or the other because the energy it took to think about it detracted from their worldly pursuits.

I was stunned. After what Jesus showed me, who could ever respect the opinions of men? I had been tying my own shoelaces for a mere year or two, but now I had to face a lifetime of being marooned in a world of fools.

Jesus then said, "People—what do they know?"

I laughed. It was clear that Jesus thought they didn't know very much.

Jesus said, "I want to remind people of the truth that you already know so well. That is why you were sent. You will be a black sheep in the world, but fear not, for I am with you always."

With all the bravado a five-year-old, toy-gun-toting Texas boy could muster, I said, "Yeah, Jesus, we'll show those guys; we'll show 'em." I had no idea what we were going to show 'em, but I was all in.

As the star's light faded, Jesus said, "And now the seed will lie dormant until the proper season."

I would not remember this night again until a quarter century later in the season of the Mule.

My loving parents raised me within the Christian church, and I attended with great excitement and curiosity. Was there anything on earth to compare with the wonders of God?

Sunday school was a joy and a challenge. My youthful mind and spirit struggled to understand the biblical tales. I was angry with Adam and Eve for eating fruit when God told them not to. Were they crazy? And this creature, the devil, certainly had a problem. Why didn't God put an end to this miserable wretch—and quickly? And how did Jesus manage to be both the Son of God and God himself at the same time? No wonder he was too busy to attend our church in person.

Of course, the Bible provided insight into spiritual mysteries, but it never went far enough to satisfy my curiosity. It was not enough for me know that there were holy angels: I wanted to know if I had my own guardian angel. It was not enough for me to know that Jesus sat on the right hand of God: I wanted to know who sat on his left. There was a restless zeal within me to know things that no man could fully explain.

I finally had to accept that—short of having God, Jesus, or a holy angel on call—my questions would never be answered while I was on earth. Yet, it was puzzling, for wouldn't men know God better if he were more forthcoming? There I went again: asking questions with no answers.

I would spend no more energy in what seemed like a fool's game.

———

As a young man, I earned a Ph.D. in psychology; I must have been sleepwalking. No man born of woman was ever more temperamentally unsuited for a profession. Mathematics made much more sense, maybe music, even manual labor—but psychology?

I didn't write the script; my life was not my own. The world would learn what the Father had to teach them.

———

I finished work for the day at the psychology clinic and blurted out to no one in particular, "I need to read the Bible."

"How strange," I thought. I shrugged my shoulders and walked outside to my pickup truck. Again I blurted, "I need to read the Bible."

I hadn't read the Bible since I was a boy. I didn't even own a Bible. So why the Bible fixation?

In a reverie, I started my five-minute drive home. Fifteen minutes later, I purchased a Bible at the bookstore across town. Okay, I got the message; I needed to read the Bible.

And what a Bible it was; the words were alive, imparting supernatural understanding. Through the guidance of the Holy Spirit, my desire to know God's mysteries was rekindled as in the days of my youth.

Soon thereafter, I began to have a strong, persistent urge to begin a private practice in psychology. I eventually made arrangements to do so. I had been carefully prepared for many years for what lay immediately ahead, but of these matters, I had no knowledge.

A mighty task awaited me: in my thirtieth year, it was time to fulfill my forgotten pact with the star.

Chapter 3

The Mule

Early November 1983

"Who is my next appointment, Diana?" I asked my secretary. "It's Mule, that twenty-five-year-old lady you tested the other day. You are going to go over the results with her now."

"Oh yeah, I remember her. Send her in."

Mule entered my office, and we exchanged light pleasantries on the way to our seats. "Mule," I said, "we weren't able to talk very much the other day, so before we go over your test results, why don't you fill me in on your current situation."

Mule said, "I don't like to talk too much about myself, because nothing can be done for me."

I asked, "What do you think needs to be done for you, Mule?"

Mule studied me, trying to gauge my intentions and take my measure. She finally said, "You are different."

I said, "I have an hour to pass; help me pass it."

Mule smiled, shrugged, and began her long tale of woe: Depression and anxiety were her constant companions. Her family of origin was quite dysfunctional. She had physical problems. She had been the victim of several violent assaults. Her life was a case study of being in harm's way.

As Mule told her story, I became less interested in what she was saying and more interested in how she was saying it. At times, she seemed frightened of me, shying away like I might strike her without warning. At other times, she seemed to want to strike me, her words often tinged with an aggressive hostility of unknown origin.

I said, "Mule, you mentioned that you live alone, but do you have any friends you can talk to?"

"Not really," she replied. "But that's fine with me because friends will just cause you pain. You can't have friends without pain."

I said, "Have you ever thought about obtaining help for some of the problems you have mentioned?"

Mule looked at me as though I were unacquainted with reality. "Help?" she spat. "There is no such thing as help. People are always saying they will help, but then they either hurt you or abandon you. Help is a deception."

By the end of our session, a different Mule had emerged, superimposed upon the original who had walked into my office. She was still herself, and yet, not. Her mouth twisted in a mocking smirk that seemed to question my right to live. A murky, light gray film clouded her eyes. Her torso tightened and recoiled from me, as though my presence threatened her existence.

I told Mule that I would be willing to meet with her again, but first, she would have to agree that help was possible. Otherwise, our efforts would be doomed to failure. I held out little hope she would agree.

Mule considered my offer for many long moments. She seemed to struggle mightily with something within her that was beyond my understanding. Finally, she gravely nodded yes. Without a word, she walked out of the office, head down, as though she had just signed her death warrant.

Early December 1983

Mule said, "The closer Christmas comes, the more I get depressed. It happens every year."

I said, "Do you have any religious beliefs, Mule?"

Mule was startled by the question. "No, not really," she replied. "Why do you ask me a question like that when I have all these other problems?"

"Simple," I replied. "Didn't you just say that you always get depressed as Christmas approaches? Christmas is a religious holiday, you know."

Mule said, "I have no religious beliefs. Does that answer your question?"

It answered one question, but it raised a more important one: why was Mule reacting to me as an embittered atheist might react to an insistent evangelist?

I asked, "So you have never believed in God at all?"

Mule looked at me with a belittling smirk and lectured me like I was a foolish child: "God is a fairy tale, just like the tooth fairy is a fairy tale. I thought everyone knew that."

"Literally a fairy tale?" I asked.

Mule said, "Of course. He is just something you imagine in your mind."

I said, "So you have never believed in God, not even as a little girl?"

"Well, I did believe in Jesus when I was very young," Mule said with a trace of wistfulness, "but where is he when you need him? Obviously, since he has never helped me, he must not exist."

I asked, "Did your family believe in God?"

Mule said, "They believed in nonsense—spiritual mediums, astrology, reincarnation, fortune-tellers—that kind of thing."

I said, "Did your family ever celebrate Christmas while you were growing up?"

Mule laughed with disdain. "You know, I once asked my mother for a Christian cross when I was little, and you know what she said? She told me to never ask for something so foolish again."

I cringed at hearing the word "foolish" associated with the cross, but pressed on. "Did you ever think to buy a cross for yourself when you got older?"

Mule gasped and shot back, "Oh, no. It's not right to buy something like that for yourself."

"Why would it be wrong, Mule?"

Mule stammered, "Well…, I don't know. It just wouldn't be right." Mule clutched at her lower left abdomen and grimaced.

I asked, "Are you in pain?"

Mule said, "Oh, it's just my colitis again."

And a most clockwork colitis it was: every time that Mule and I seemed to make progress during our sessions, she experienced disabling abdominal pains. Now that we were talking about God, the pains were getting worse.

I continued, "So you are telling me that you once believed in Jesus and wanted a cross, but now you don't have the same desire?"

"You know, it's weird," Mule replied with desperate undertones, "but I know I am in big trouble if I get a cross. That's crazy, isn't it? But I am sure if I had a cross, I would be in big trouble."

I said, "That doesn't answer my question exactly, Mule. Do you still find yourself wanting a cross?"

"I think so," she said timidly, "but can we talk about something else? My stomach hurts."

For the moment, I dropped the matter. Mule's life had given her little reason to have faith in the existence of a caring, loving God. My job was to help her with her depression, not convert her to Christianity. Still, I was struck by the extreme sensitivity she had displayed towards God and the cross.

But there seemed to be more important issues at hand than religion. I turned my mind back to Mule's depression and the coming holidays. Although I was generally opposed to the use of medications for most psychological disorders, Mule's discomfort was extreme, and her hope, nonexistent.

"Let's get you on some medications, Mule," I suggested. "They might give you some temporary relief."

Late December 1983

Mule said, "My symptoms are getting worse. I've even begun to have strong thoughts about killing myself."

I asked, "What are you thinking about right before these thoughts come?"

"Usually nothing," she said. "The thoughts come from nowhere. It is almost like someone is placing them in my mind."

"That's not a good sign, Mule," I said without further commitment.

"Wait till you hear this, then: sometimes I hear voices too."

I said, "Describe them."

"They are children's voices," she said, "and they sing my name over and over. It is not singing really—more like a chant. They chant, 'Mule, come play; Mule come play in the dark.'"

I noticed a long scratch on Mule's arm and asked, "How did that get there?"

Mule appeared embarrassed and shrugged. "I have no idea."

I said, "It is okay to tell me, Mule."

"No, really," she insisted. "I have no idea. It happens from time to time, but I have no memory of doing it to myself."

I said, "Mule, given these symptoms, I am concerned about your safety. Maybe you should go to the hospital for a while, just until things get a bit more stable."

"Oh, I can't go to the hospital, because I will die there," she shot back with a horrified expression.

"Die?" I asked.

Mule said, "I just heard a voice say that if I go to the hospital, I will die there."

I said, "Mule, I think the hospital is the best place for you right now. Since you live alone, no one is around to watch you at night. That worries me. The hospital is only a temporary thing—a precaution."

"I refuse to go to the hospital," Mule said. "It was hard enough to come here and see you."

Short of leaving her to struggle on her own—and this I was unwilling to do—I could only continue seeing her on an outpatient basis.

Early January 1984

I awakened with a compulsion to buy Mule a Christian cross. And why not buy her a cross? She needed all the help she could get. If the cross offended her, she could either refuse it or throw it away. All I knew was that I had to buy her a cross. I purchased a simple cross necklace and brought it to our next scheduled meeting.

"I have a gift for you," I said to Mule as I handed her the cross, tucked away in a small white box.

Mule stared at me blankly. "This is not right," she finally said. "I should not accept this."

I was certain she knew what it was. I asked, "Accept what, Mule: a gift—or this particular gift? You don't have to keep it, but I think you might want to see what it is first."

Mule reluctantly opened the box to reveal the gleaming gold cross framed by a white cotton backing. She gasped. I could not tell whether she was touched by the gift or pained by it.

Mule's eyes moistened, and after an uncomfortably long pause, she finally uttered a whispered, "Thank you."

Deep within Mule's trapped soul, a shadowy, sinister spirit had been contradicted. Evil could dismiss any challenge that did not threaten its existence, but the gauntlet of the cross could not be ignored.

<hr />

As Mule began to wear her cross necklace regularly, her condition deteriorated even further.

The content of Mule's dreams became even more bizarre than usual: snakes would crawl over her lifeless body, even while a part of her remained alive inside of it; she would do violent harm to me, usually with a carving knife; hideous beings would torment her in a place of fiery heat and pitch blackness.

Mule also developed daytime blackouts that were alarming to both of us. Sometimes, she would awaken to find sleeping pills or a sharp carving knife in her hand. At other times, she would be coiled in the fetal position, rocking herself back and forth. She had vague memories of talking to a person clothed in black. Amazingly, she spoke to the black-clad figure in the voice of a preschool child.

I had worked with a number of individuals having Mule's symptoms, and I had studied many more. In my experience, traditional psychological diagnosis was of no value in these cases. What good was it to call someone "schizophrenic" or some other label if the label gave no clue as to the origin of the problem, and hence, its treatment? To name something properly, one must understand what is being named. This was a puzzle with a very large, yet flagrantly elusive missing piece.

I again suggested to Mule that she enter the hospital. She reluctantly agreed, for her symptoms now scared her more than the hospital. The only hope was that we might learn more about the cause of her problems.

Indeed, we would.

When I visited Mule in the hospital, I barely recognized the corpse-like figure before me.

"What is going on with you, Mule?" I asked. "I've never seen you like this before, and I've seen you in pretty bad shape."

Mule managed a weak smile and joked, "I don't know—you tell me—you're the doctor."

I shrugged and said, "I'm glad to see you remembered to wear your cross necklace."

Mule said, "Lot of good it's doing me, huh?"

Suddenly, something caught my eye. On Mule's left collarbone, I saw what looked to be a thumbnail-sized scar in the shape of a cross, tilted at about a fifteen-degree angle.

I pointed to the area and asked, "What's that scar, Mule? I've never noticed it before."

She looked at me blankly. "What scar?"

"This scar," I said, as I tapped it with my index finger. "It's a scar in the shape of a cross."

Mule grabbed a mirror from the bedside table and observed the scar. "That's scary. That's the first time I've ever seen it. Where did it come from?"

I said, "I don't know—don't even have a plausible guess at the moment."

Mule said, "Something else mysterious happened last night. As I was about to fall asleep, I was thinking of Jesus and whether he was real or not, and I felt someone kissing me on the forehead. I didn't see anything, but I sure felt it. It didn't scare me though, like you might think. What do you think about that?"

I said, "I'll have to think about that for a while. I'm not sure what it means right now."

Mule said, "Sometimes I feel like I should just take my cross off and throw it away. But something else tells me to hold on to it because it is my only hope. But it seems like things have gotten really out of hand since I started wearing it. My stomach is killing me. If help is like this, I'm certain it will eventually kill me."

I asked, "What do the hospital doctors say is wrong with you?"

Mule said, "They say a lot of things: they say I have a thinking disorder, and that I am depressed, and that I may have a chemical imbalance of some sort. You know, it's funny, but I know they really have no idea how to fix me and are just saying those things so they can be good doctors in their own minds. The pills they have given me haven't helped at all."

I said, "Maybe they will work given some time."

Mule looked at me with a puzzled expression. "Did you just laugh at me?"

"Laugh at you?"

Mule said, "I distinctly heard a sick laugh. I must really be crazy."

With a sad sigh, I said, "Don't worry about it now, Mule."

I looked over to the empty bed adjacent to Mule's and noticed an open Bible, face down on the pillow. "Where's your roommate, Mule?"

Mule said, "I don't know, but she's been real nice to me. She's trying to teach me some things about God. But just when I feel good enough to listen, my pains will suddenly get worse."

"Rest for now, Mule," I said. "When you get better, we will get you a Bible and you can read all you want."

As I prepared to leave, Mule asked, "Do you know if this hospital has a priest? For some strange reason, I want to talk to a priest."

Before I could answer, Mule released a deep groan and nearly fainted from a sudden, sharp pain in her lower abdomen.

The hospital chaplain, a Catholic priest, heard of Mule's extreme difficulties and stopped by for a visit.

"Having troubles, huh?" the priest asked as he sat on the edge of her bed.

Mule could only nod. As the priest entered the room, she had suddenly started to feel worse—if indeed that was possible.

"Well, everyone has troubles from time to time," the priest said with a humorous tone of voice. "Even priests have trouble at times, would you believe?"

Mule watched silently as the priest pulled his own bottle of medication from the pocket of his trousers. She appreciated the priest being there, but she hurt too much to smile.

The priest noticed Mule's struggle and quickly became serious. "Don't you worry, young lady, because things will get better. God will make it better."

Suddenly, a question bolted into Mule's mind; she did not know where it came from, but she just had to ask the priest: "Is there really such a thing as the devil?"

"You bet there is," the priest quickly replied, "and don't you ever let anybody tell you any different."

Mule said, "How do you know for sure? How do you know it's not just your imagination?"

The wise priest said, "You ask me how I know for sure. Given your condition, how is it that you do not know for sure?"

As her spasms intensified, Mule clutched at her lower abdomen.

The priest reassured, "I understand, young lady. I'll come back later when you feel a little more like talking."

As the priest walked away, Mule felt the pain ease ever so slightly, as though an unseen hand had momentarily relaxed its relentless grip.

Chapter 4

Halo of Protection

February 1984

My mother blurted, "Jesus visited me this morning."
"Yes, mom, Jesus is always with us. Would you please pass the orange juice?"

She said, "No, you don't understand. I actually saw him."

I stared at her. "Mom, do we have to adjust the dosage on your pain medications again?"

"No, it's not like that," she said. "First thing this morning as I woke up, Jesus was standing beside my bed. He had a message for me and part of it concerns you. He told me to write down his words and to make sure you read it when you came over. He was very emphatic about you reading it. He said you would know what to make of it, so you can read for yourself."

I accepted the offered notebook and read Jesus' words:

> Wait, please. You were in pain this week and sought help for your pain. I know you were refused help. Those responsible will walk in your shoes, and they will fit very tightly.
>
> Be not afraid; there is Someone more powerful than doctors who does understand. Whatever decision you

make concerning this matter will be the right decision. Remember: I know your decisions before you make them; I guide your decisions. Sleep on it and when you wake up, you will know the answer.

Remember: Whenever you pray, I answer you; but sometimes I don't answer in a way that you approve. Sometimes, you have to wait for an answer.

People—what do they know? *(My mother laughs.)* It's good to see you laugh; I haven't seen you laugh in a long time. Farmer is smarter than you are; he laughs more than you do. He has the ability, like all smart people, to concentrate on what is really important.

Farmer and Miriam *(a family friend)* are my way of showing you how much I love you. I have molded Farmer into a very fine young man, and I have molded Miriam into a very fine young woman. I chose them because you love them, and their loving you meant just as much as if I was there with you. When Farmer was a babe, I placed him in your arms; I have placed him in your arms again.

There waits a place for all three of you in my Kingdom, where there is love, joy, and happiness eternally. Farmer and Miriam will have peace, security, and happiness throughout their earthly lives also. I have placed a halo of protection around the heads of Farmer and Miriam, but no one can see it.

Before I leave, remember that love is the greatest way to treat pain. Love will do more for you than all hospitals and doctors ever could; love always comes through. Peace, my child, I am always there.

I read Jesus' words several times, trying to absorb all the lessons. It made perfect sense within the context of my mother's situation, except for "halo of protection." What was a halo of protection and why did I need one? Why now? Even stranger, why did Miriam need one and not my mother? I felt it had something to do with Mule, but the full meaning was hidden from me.

Who could fathom the ways of God? I would never understand why he gave people like me so many blessings, and people like Mule, so few.

<hr/>

The devil? How odd for Mule to ask the hospital chaplain about the devil. She had trouble enough accepting the reality of God, much less the devil.

The subject of the devil had not been part of my orthodox psychological training. If a client reported to have heard or seen the devil or Satan or a demon, it was automatically regarded by teaching faculty as a delusion or hallucination, a symptom of a confused mind. There was never any serious suggestion that Satan might be a real being who interfered in people's thoughts, emotions, and behaviors.

Yet now, even though I accepted the reality of Satan because Jesus had spoken of him in the Bible, I had no idea if he was responsible for Mule's problems. I was only certain that he did not have a tail and horns—I was entirely too rational to believe that.

As I studied the biblical passages on Satan, I could not find definitive proof of his involvement in Mule's problems. However, my intuition strongly testified that it *was* possible. I tried to imagine more mundane explanations; yet the more I tried to discard the Satan hypothesis, the more it returned to my mind. Intellectual honesty would not allow me to rule out the possibility of Satan's involvement given the facts of Mule's situation.

Mule had finally been released from the hospital—much the worse for wear. She had apparently gone as far as human skill and knowledge would take her—not very far. Yet I could not rest until all possibilities for helping her had been exhausted. I greatly admired her courage and persistence in the face of wretched suffering. If by some remote chance Satan was actually involved in her problems, I would do everything I could to assist her.

I reviewed the situation with Mule and was frank with her about my doubts that traditional psychological methods would solve her problems. Though I offered her the opportunity to seek help from someone else, she insisted on working only with me; yet in good conscience, I could no longer continue with my previous focus. Mule and I agreed to seek a spiritual resolution to her difficulties; for in truth, no other course could any longer be justified.

March–May 1984

Real knowledge of Satan is difficult to come by. I found a small number of writings that emphasized the reality of Satan and testified to his ability to affect a person's emotional, physical, and spiritual well-being. These writings, though simplistic, were heartfelt and most welcome. Yet there was little guidance about what to do in these instances besides prayer or perhaps a ritual exorcism. There were no writings that I found that gave me the detailed guidance I was looking for.

I then focused on finding an experienced individual who could advise me on Satan. Unfortunately, the chaplain whom Mule had befriended in the hospital was not able to be more specific as to how I should proceed with her. Despite my best research efforts, I was unable to find any meaningful help.

The advice I received, from both the Christian and secular realms, ran the gamut. Some advisors suggested that Satan was not an actual being, but the impersonal force of evil that lurked in the hearts of all men. I was not even sure what this meant, but I was certain it would not help me to help Mule. Some advisors suggested that Satan, though real, did not work in the ways that I had described. In their minds, he could not cause physical or psychological symptoms, only spiritual ones (as though they were mutually exclusive). Some advisors, a greedier lot, suggested that before Mule could be helped, a large financial contribution needed to be made to their so-called ministries. Yes, with the simple purchase of a "prayer cloth" or other such icon, the blessings of Heaven would pour down upon Mule. Some advisors, ones not particularly cognizant of their personal safety, even insisted that I needed their help because I had lost my grip on reality. To sum: there was no room at the inn—Mule and I were on our own in the world of men.

The content of Mule's sessions during these weeks varied according to which Mule happened to attend. One Mule was very gentle and childlike, with a consuming desire to know more about God. The other Mule exhibited a wide range of foul moods and behaviors, the only consistency being a vicious contempt towards God (and me). In essence, there was a pro-God Mule and an anti-God Mule, and she had no control over which one she would be at any given moment.

There was a profound difference in how the two Mules responded to spiritual stimuli. The pro-God Mule was able to read the Bible aloud without any difficulties; she never stuttered when pronouncing Jesus' name; she remembered and understood the basic Gospel message; she always wore her cross necklace; she felt hope for the future; and most importantly, she had an intense desire to please God.

To the contrary, the anti-God Mule experienced perceptual distortions and nausea when reading the Bible; she resisted saying Jesus' name, and if she did try, she stuttered; she forgot the basic Gospel message and could not have cared less; she forgot to wear her cross; she had no hope for her future; and most revealingly, she displayed a contempt towards God himself.

To my layman's knowledge, this evidence strongly pointed to Satan's involvement in Mule's problems. Yet where was I to go from here? The experts in this field, if there were any, would not take me seriously enough to investigate the matter. Even if Satan had appeared and told me that he was responsible for all of Mule's problems, I would not have known how to proceed. I felt a great responsibility towards Mule and a great frustration at my inability to help her in the way she needed to be helped.

Mule did not have much time left. Her psychotic symptoms were becoming even more frequent and intense. She was sliding into darkness. Before long, she would either abandon her sessions or her life. In my mind, it was a miracle she had even made it this far.

Where was God? Was it possible that Mule had sought a God who would not deliver?

Lurking in the dark shadows of Mule's soul, the evil inhabitant gleefully watched the chaotic confusion. There was nothing that pleased him more than torturing God's children. Over the years, he had done a masterful job on the pitiful woman, and now her earthly helper had provided an entertaining diversion. Humans were so stupid; they had no clue.

But the evil inhabitant was beginning to worry: Although the game had been fun, if he waited too long, God might deliver her. He had seen it happen many times before.

Now was the perfect time to spring the trap and deliver the deceived prey to his outcast father.

Part III

Luther's Game

(May 27, 1984 – July 7, 1984)

I know all about Luther. Luther is going to lose the game.

– Jesus

Chapter 5

My Name is Luther

May 27, 1984

Mule was hopelessly tangled in the briers of suicidal despair. The initial brier, an isolated depressive thought, would have been quickly plucked by a stronger spirit. Yet Mule's unwitting delay had encouraged it to grow more bold and persistent. Now it had taken root in her emotions and mercilessly choked the will to live. Mule's only defense was to force herself into bed, away from potentially lethal devices.

Intertwined with the bedroom shadows, a fiendish figure watched the pathetic scene. He liked to play games: one of his favorites was to place depressive thoughts into Mule's unsuspecting mind. She was especially fun to play with, for not only would she accept the depressive thoughts, she would also feel guilty about causing them.

The fiendish figure shook his head at the utter stupidity of mankind. Would they never understand even the most basic of realities? Thoughts could be self-generated, but they could also be placed in the mind from Above or Below. The Bible was so clear on the matter, how could anyone miss it?

The Apostle Peter was an excellent example of the principle: To be sure, he had thoughts of his own creation, according to his God-given soul and intelligence; yet had not God himself placed the thought in Peter's mind that Jesus was the Christ? And had not Satan placed the thought in Peter's mind that Jesus must not die on the cross? How then could men so consistently believe they created all their own thoughts?

The five-foot-tall evil fiend, his figure completely covered by a black, hooded monk's robe, stealthily approached Mule's bedside. He would not share her with anyone, especially not God. It was now time to play the ultimate game with his human toy.

In a raspy, whispering voice, the fiend spoke, "My dear, I know you are very unhappy, and I would like to help. I can take your pain away very quickly and easily."

Mule was entranced by the talking robe that stood beside her bed. It seemed like an old friend. She asked, "How can you take my pain away?"

"If you will merely kill yourself," the fiend explained, "there will be no more pain."

Mule asked, "What's your name, sir?"

The fiend said, "I've always kept my name a secret from you, my dear. But as long as you call Jesus by his name, I guess it would be okay for you to call me by mine. My name is Luther."

"Lucifer?" Mule asked. "I've heard about you."

"No, my dear," the fiend corrected. "I'm Luther. Lucifer is my father."

Mule asked, "Well, what will happen to me if I kill myself, Luther?"

Luther said, "Why, of course, you will go to Heaven, my dear. It's really very peaceful there. Let me show you."

In the next moment, Mule stood on the grassy banks of a magnificent lake and surveyed the Great Mystery. How delightful! Heaven was the fullest bloom of nature—natural to the extreme—supernatural.

Shafts of tall meadow grasses, mixed with delicate white flowers on extra long stems, bowed in unison to greet Mule's arrival. Yes, they did; they bowed in unison, as though greeting royalty. The animals of the nearby forest gathered about and spoke their welcomes in animal languages; Mule understood perfectly and gave her regards in her own.

And, oh, the colors of Heaven: Greens vibrated with life; blues elicited calm; whites conferred purity. Earthly colors made a pale palette by comparison.

Mule looked to the lake's opposite shore and saw an array of the tallest spruce trees with perfectly triangulated tops. The tree trunks had the deep texture of fresh modeling clay. One trunk, with intricate gnarls on its surface, held Mule's attention for several long moments.

What was this? Mule could not believe her eyes. As she continued to focus on the tree, she simultaneously saw the tree from its opposite side. How could she be on both sides of the tree? As she focused even more intently, she began to see the tree from all sides, a 360-degree panorama. As more time passed and concentration deepened, she even began to see the tree from inside the tree. Oh, my! Mule was simultaneously inside and outside of the tree's boundaries, examining the tree. In contrast to earth's three dimensions, Heaven had unlimited dimensions for God's children to sample at will. The purity of perception was astounding.

At the height of Mule's reverie, she was brusquely returned to the misery of her earthly life. She would gladly do whatever was necessary to return to Heaven if she could only find out how.

Luther knew the power of the bait he had dangled before Mule. Of course, as a fallen angel, he did not now have access to Heaven; yet he was well able to project his memory of how it was before he fell. Now he hoped the deceptive vision would trick Mule into eternal damnation. In Luther's mind, this was a deserved return on a twenty-year investment.

The manipulation of human perception was a time-honored trick of Luther's brethren. There were, of course, normal human dreams during nighttime slumber, where the mind's natural currents wove pictures with the imagination. However, visions were entirely another thing: they were much more vivid in imagery than dreams; and just like thoughts, they could come from Above or Below.

Luther's favorite use of visions was in the so-called "night terrors" of vulnerable youth. It was great fun to show sleeping children the horrors of Hell. But it was even more fun when doctors would give drugs to suppress the terrors; or better still, when parents punished the children for having an overactive imagination. These confusions really made the game worthwhile.

Luther was also quite fond of the "Jesus made me do it" vision. In this game, Luther would create a picture of Jesus in the mind of a human soul weakened by drugs, hatred, or some such evil. Then, "Jesus" would tell the soul that he must kill all the members of his family, or the wicked infidels, or whomever. The deceived soul, believing he was doing something commanded by the Lord, would then carry out the dastardly deed.

What made this game especially fun was not so much the murders themselves, but the subsequent publicity. Under the focus of the media, for all to see and hear, the murderer would confess that he committed the crime because Jesus told him to do it. Deceived onlookers would nudge each other in the ribs and swear off any involvement in religious matters. There was no better publicity for Satan's kingdom.

Luther knew that deception afforded Evil the best of both worlds: if visions were from Below, they would often accomplish their wicked purpose; if visions were from Above (as for the noble Jeanne d'Arc), who would believe it? Yes, deception was the spice of life.

Luther now sprung his well-crafted trap on Mule, still captivated by her vision of Heaven. He asked, "Would you like to go to Heaven permanently, my dear?"

"Oh, yes," Mule exulted. "Can you help me get there, Luther?"

Luther said, "Well, you have to kill yourself first. Those are the rules we all play by. But then I will be most pleased to take you. You won't ever have to be unhappy again."

Mule said, "Oh, thank you, Luther."

The fallen angel reached out his robed arm and brushed Mule on the cheek. "You see, my dear, I'm your friend, and I really hate to see you suffer."

Mule said, "You must be my friend, Luther, if you can help me get to Heaven."

Luther said, "Yes, I will even help you to kill yourself. I know just what to do. I have lots of experience in these matters."

Luther escorted Mule from her bedroom into the kitchen. "Let's take a look at the knives," he suggested. Luther pointed to the cutlery drawer and it slowly opened to reveal Mule's knife set. Luther shook with ecstasy and shrieked, "These beauties will kill you for sure!"

Luther selected a knife and handed it to Mule. "Here, use this carving knife," he said. "It's my personal favorite of the ones you have. The seven-inch blade works wonders. So go ahead and kill yourself with style."

Mule said, "But my family might miss me."

Luther laughed. "Miss you? They gave you two identical sets of knives—can't you take a hint? It's a clear message that they want you dead, or else why the overkill? So there's nothing holding you here."

Mule said, "What do I do?"

Luther said, "Just get on your knees, hold the knife on the floor with the blade sticking up, and then fall on it. It's like you are praying and then sacrifice your life to God. Quite dramatic, even poetic, I think."

Mule shuddered. "Oh, no," she said. "I don't really like sharp things. And anyway, it would be too messy."

Luther scoffed, "What difference does it make what you look like? You won't be taking your body with you."

Mule said, "But I have to take it with me, because I don't even know who I am now. So how will I know then if I don't have my body with me?"

Luther said, "It's simple, my dear: you won't need your body because it will be too hot to wear."

Hot? Heaven had not been hot. Luther's verbal slip completely escaped Mule's notice.

With mock concern, Luther placed his arm around Mule's shoulder and steered her into the bathroom. "Maybe you could hang yourself from the shower rod. Many people choose this route to Heaven."

"Do you think it is strong enough?" Mule inquired. "It's not very sturdy."

Luther sighed, "Perhaps you are right, my dear."

Luther beckoned towards the mirrored door of the medicine cabinet and it swung open to reveal a potpourri of pills. "What about all these pills?" he asked. "I know you like pills. Perhaps with a cocktail, they will do the trick. I've recommended this method many times before, especially with women concerned with their looks. You know, a good friend will always help you to find the right way to do things."

Mule shook her head and said, "No, I've tried that before, and I got real sick, and I didn't die."

With exasperation seeping into his voice, Luther lectured: "My dear, I don't know why you bungled your previous suicide attempts, because I took away your fear. How easy can I make it for you? I can't make you kill yourself, because I don't have that power. Only you have the power to actually kill yourself. I can only try to convince you that it is the right thing to do. But as soon as you decide how you want to do it, I'll come for you. I can wait for you to decide."

Luther calmed himself so as not to frighten his prey. "My dear, you need to remember that I'm the only real friend you have. God is way too busy with other people to take the time to help you. And anyway, you are bad; God doesn't help bad people."

Mule meekly protested, "But I want to be good. I'm trying to get some help so that I will be good."

Luther said, "Yes, I know all about that man you are seeing. He's a wicked, wicked man. He doesn't really care about you. He only says nice things to you to make you well so you won't take up any more of his time. I know you'll end up coming with me forever." Luther then disappeared into the shadows.

Mule felt disoriented: Why was she staring into the bathroom medicine cabinet with a sharp knife in her hand? Would she ever stop talking in her sleep and having these bizarre dreams?

Chapter 6

The Evil Chorus

May 28, 1984

There were no remaining doubts in my mind about Satan's involvement in Mule's problems.

The Bible taught of Evil's history: In a time before man's creation, Heaven was populated by hosts of holy angels, created by God to serve him. The angel Lucifer, also known as Satan or the devil, was the greatest of these in beauty, power, and knowledge, behind only God and Jesus in Heaven's hierarchy. Lucifer's splendor eventually filled him with arrogant pride, and he sought to place himself above God on Heaven's throne. A group of angels followed Lucifer in his doomed rebellion, and God subsequently cast them out of Heaven. Jesus often encountered these fallen angels, also called demons or evil spirits, in his earthly walk. The fallen angel Luther was now trying to deceive Mule into Hell.

Late that evening, as Mule lay in bed, Luther suddenly appeared, again hidden by his monk's robe.

Luther scolded: "My dear, you are a foolish, foolish girl. The wicked man is teasing you about help, because your time is running out. If you need help to kill yourself, I could arrange an accident. And watch out what you eat, because you wouldn't taste the poison."

A chorus of children's voices abruptly called to Mule in chilling, atonal unison: "Mule, come play; Mule come play in the dark."

Mule shook with fear. She asked, "Who is that, Luther? I've heard them before."

Luther explained, "The many happy voices you hear belong to my children. Their souls belong to me because I helped them to kill themselves, just as I will help you."

Mule asked, "Why are they calling me?"

"They just want you to come play with them," Luther said. "Think about joining them, because you will have just as good a time as they are having."

Mule said, "My hospital doctors said it was crazy to hear voices. They said I was out of touch with reality."

Luther snickered, "Perhaps they are not aware of all the possibilities, my dear."

Over time, the persistent voices wore down Mule's resistance. Luther asked, "Are you ready to kill yourself and join them, my dear?"

Mule mildly protested, "I'm too tired to think about it right now. I just want to sleep. I can't make up my mind because I am so tired." She closed her eyes in the hope that Luther would go away and take his children with him.

"Well, my dear, you rest for now," Luther said with false concern. "Of course, you are quite right that you need some strength to kill yourself. But I will come back for you later, because you are very special to me. You have to come with me, and then all your pain will be gone."

Luther's raspy wheeze suddenly ceased. Mule breathed a sigh of relief; yet before opening her eyes, she waited for several minutes to make sure Luther was gone. She heard nothing and slowly opened an eyelid. As she did, she was startled to see the robe's hood perched inches from her face.

Luther burst into raucous laughter at the deception. He slowly raised up, straightened out his arm, and very gradually extended his index finger out from beneath the robe's sleeve. Mule stared hypnotically at the yellowish-orange, mangled digit that enticed her to follow.

The next thing Mule remembered, it was morning. She felt the sting of long fingernail scratches on either arm. Her wrists were striped with shallow cuts. Next to the bed, a razor blade, splattered with blood, lay on the carpet.

Luther did enjoy his games.

Chapter 7

Light of a Different Kind

May 29, 1984

 Mule described Luther's latest visit to me. "Why doesn't God help me? Are you sure he really exists?"

"Yes, I'm sure," I said. "Jesus even visited my mother while you were in the hospital."

Mule said, "Why doesn't he visit me, then? I thought you said that Jesus loved me. If this is love, I don't want any part of it."

"It is difficult to explain with words, Mule," I said, "but I know that Jesus loves you specifically. I sense it."

"Well, where is Jesus now? You said there was such a thing as help, but where is it now?"

I said, "Oh, Jesus will help you; he will. He won't let Luther continue bullying you."

With the neediest voice I had ever heard, Mule asked, "Are you going to abandon me now?"

"Of course not, Mule," I said.

But the situation was beyond human hands. Without Jesus' help, Mule would soon be joining Luther's hellish chorus.

For the third consecutive evening, the persistent Luther stalked Mule. "Come with me, my dear," he enticed.

In the next instant, Mule found herself strapped to a multicolored parachute, floating lazily downward in a sky of brilliant blue. She looked down and recognized the topographical landmarks of Heaven, and she was filled with peace.

Luther called out, "Look over here." Mule was startled to see Luther, in his own parachute, floating next to her.

Luther stroked the cords of his parachute and said, "People are like the cords on this parachute: they bind you and tangle you up. Yes, you have to watch out for people. When you get too close to them, they hurt you."

Suddenly, Luther's favorite carving knife materialized in the sky. How had the knife gotten to Heaven? Luther fixed his eyes upon the knife and directed it through the air into Mule's grasp.

Luther urged, "Go on and cut the cords on your parachute. Freedom is so releasing. And you know that you need to be free."

Mule considered the proposition: If she did sever the cords, perhaps she would fall to Heaven painlessly and permanently. On the other hand, she might not. She had experienced enough pain in her life and would not risk more.

At the instant Mule made her decision, she found herself standing on the second-floor balcony of her apartment with the carving knife at her feet. What had happened to Heaven? She did not see Luther beside her and turned to go inside the adjoining bedroom.

Luther cried out from the darkness, "I'm over here." Mule turned and saw the unsupported demon treading air on the opposite side of the balcony railing. "See, I can do miracles too, just like Jesus can," he boasted. "Come on out here. You won't fall. I'll hold you up."

Unknown to Mule, she had been perched on the edge of her balcony railing as she was "parachuting" with Luther. If she had raised her arms to sever the parachute cords, she would have lost her balance and plummeted to the concrete below. She knew Luther would not hold her up if she went to him. But that did not concern her. She *was* concerned, however, that the fall would not be fatal; and thus, she would have to suffer more pain.

Mule reasoned with Luther, "I don't think it would kill me even if I did fall. It's probably not high enough."

"Maybe you are right, my dear," Luther said. "But do give some thought to jumping off something that is high enough. While you are falling, you feel so free. And after you land, you are."

Luther escorted Mule back inside her apartment and nodded towards a neatly wrapped package on the bedroom nightstand. "Go ahead and open it," he urged.

Mule reached over, removed the wrapping, and discovered an antique handgun. The handle was made of pure ivory with an intricately etched design. Mule said, "It's very pretty, Luther."

"I know you have always liked delicate things," Luther said with hypocritical care, "so now you can go ahead and kill yourself with style."

Mule winced and said, "Oh, no, that would be too messy, just like with the knives."

Luther signaled with a wave of his hand, and his children began to chant, "Mule, come play with us; come play with us forever."

Mule searched for the children in the darkness of her home. She asked, "Where are they, Luther?"

Luther said, "Oh, they are just playing in the dark like they always do, my dear."

Mule said, "I don't like the dark; it scares me."

The sick evil of Luther's mind could not be contained: "Oh, there is a light where they are playing, my dear, but it is a light of a different kind. Why don't you join them? The firelight is so romantic, and I know you have been wondering what love is all about."

For the moment, Luther had wasted enough of his energy on the woman. Before leaving for other adventures, he issued a stern warning: "Be sure not to tell the wicked man anything about tonight, or I'll hurt you. He is going to abandon you just like everyone else. I'll see to that; and believe me, I have my ways. And anyway, how could you be so stupid as to believe what the wicked man's mother says about Jesus when you've never even met her?"

May 30, 1984

Mule was in desperate straits. Some action had to be taken immediately, and I was the only one in a position to take it. I directed my thoughts toward God and earnestly sought guidance.

After waiting many long moments, no answer was forthcoming. My mind drifted to thoughts of my childhood. I tried to bring my thoughts back to the problem at hand: this was no time for fanciful thoughts of times past. Yet my mind would not stay focused on the present.

The picture in my mind seemed frivolous at first glance. What was I doing as a young child sitting on the front lawn of my family's home? I followed my line of sight to the radiant star sparkling overhead. Suddenly, I remembered. A smile crossed my face as I felt the feelings of that time so long ago. What a funny thing to think about after so many years, especially now.

What had happened that night? Oh, yes, Jesus had impressed upon me the utter folly of man. He had asked me to help remind his children of the truth of life, without specifying how that was to be accomplished. The path would be exceedingly difficult, and would win me no popularity contests, but Jesus promised to be with me always. Surely, this was just the imagination of a little boy.

Yet as I considered all that had happened, an amazing scenario began to unfold: What if freeing Mule from Luther was related to Jesus' visit on that long-ago night? And what if my compulsion to read the Bible had been meant to prepare me? And what if Jesus' assurances of salvation and a divine halo of protection had been meant to strengthen me? As incredible as it sounded, it seemed that I had been called, prepared, and assured protection for the task of freeing Mule from her evil shadow.

My soul was overwhelmed by the now obvious reality: there actually was a Satan, and demons who followed him, and a Hell they lived in, and people they tormented.

My education had just begun: there would be more incredible revelations to come, quite beyond the capacity of a man to imagine.

Chapter 8

First Confrontation

May 31, 1984

The Bible taught that an intercessor must take authority over a demon in the name of Jesus. It was by Jesus' name and the Holy Spirit that a believer could lawfully command evil spirit to depart. Therefore, the next time I sensed Luther's presence, I resolved to command him to confront me and then dispatch him by my authority as a believer in Jesus. The opportunity soon came.

"Mule," I said, "Jesus will help you to get rid of Luther, just as he helped others with this same problem."

Mule stiffened and her eyes fixed in bewilderment. She stuttered, "But where is Je…, Jes…, Ysh…?"

My adrenaline began to flow as I sensed what was ahead. I urged Mule, "Try to say Jesus' name again."

Mule rapidly transformed into the anti-God Mule. With sullen contempt, she said, "I don't want to."

I quickly moved my chair next to Mule's and secured her wrists with my hands. She muttered excitedly, "I'm leaving, far away, hot, no. Don't let me go. Don't let me go." [AUTHOR'S NOTE: *Many demons are not overtly violent. However, sometimes physical restraint is necessary to prevent the demon from hurting either its victim (usually its first instinct) or the intercessor. The restraint is protective and defensive in nature (of both victim and intercessor), never offensive. The intercessor cannot "beat the devil" out of the victim, though the demon will try to bait a trap for the intercessor to try. This principle is more fully explained later in the book.*]

I then spoke the words that came to me: "Luther, in the name of Jesus, I command you to leave her alone and confront me."

Mule's body gave a slight jerk. She composed herself and calmly replied, "But no one is here. Everything is okay."

I paused for a moment. If everything were okay, I was physically restraining Mule for no purpose. Momentarily, I felt quite the fool.

Yet something else came to mind. I said, "Mule, I didn't ask you whether anyone was there or not. Sort of a peculiar way of responding to me, don't you think?"

The reply was a twisted, mocking smirk. It was a game of cat and mouse, but which one was I?

I took a deep breath and said, "Luther, in the name of Jesus, I command you to stop hiding behind her personality and confront me."

Mule's body slumped into a heap over the arm of the reclining chair. Her facial features distended slightly. I gently shook her body, but couldn't rouse her. What now? I placed my hands on either side of her head and searched for signs of her presence.

A sly, contemptuous grin mocked my search. I peeled back Mule's eyelids and was startled to see only the whites of her eyes staring back vacantly. Something was definitely present, but it wasn't Mule. I again secured her wrists.

I said, "Luther, in the name of Jesus, I command you to quit hiding and come forth."

Suddenly, with inhuman strength, Mule's wrists pulled away from my grasp. Her face contorted into a queer position that defied earthly physics. Her hair soaked through with sweat. A blast of noise, presumably male, shot forth from her mouth, "No, wicked man, she is mine." I was finally in the sickening presence of Luther, who now fully possessed the container of Mule's body.

I grabbed Mule's wrists and commanded, "Luther, be gone in the name of Jesus."

In return, Luther struggled mightily to break free of my grip.

I repeated, "Luther, be gone in the name of Jesus."

In reply, Luther shouted threats.

Something was terribly wrong. Why hadn't Luther gone? I thought his disposal would simply be a matter of giving the command in the name of Jesus, but I now found myself engaged in a spiritual and physical endurance test. Yet even though Luther struggled against me with great resolve, in the chair he remained; for I was filled with a supernatural strength of unknown origin.

Luther hissed, "I don't like your friend, wicked man."

"She doesn't like you either," I said.

Luther replied, "Not her—the Powerful One. If the Powerful One was not helping you right now, I would kill you."

The blundering Luther had unintentionally bolstered my confidence. Jesus was, indeed, aware of the situation and helping me at this very moment. There were many things I had to learn, but I knew nothing could overcome Jesus.

"She belongs to Jesus," I said with heightened authority.

Luther sneered, "You'll be sorry, wicked man. We will make you very sorry. We all know you are going to go to Heaven when you die, but don't forget we can make your earthly life very miserable. She is going to be with us, though, and there is nothing you can do to stop us."

"Let her go, Luther," I said angrily. "In the name of Jesus, I command you to let her go."

Luther snarled, "Her biggest mistake was accepting the cross. We will get back at her when she least expects it. She won't be able to call on Jesus without your help."

I continued to pray, and Luther gradually weakened. I said, "Luther, be gone in the name of Jesus. You are not going to do anything that God does not allow."

Luther departed with a rush. Mule's body went limp and she again slumped over onto the cushioned arm of her chair. I lifted her eyelids and saw her pupils attempting to focus. After regaining her senses, she stared at me in bewilderment.

I asked, "Where have you been, Mule?"

She shuddered. "I went someplace where it was hot and dark. I've been there before, but I never want to go there again."

I said, "Do you know what happened while you were gone?"

"Yes, I think so," Mule said. "I heard your voice, even though it sounded very far away, and you were fighting with Luther. It's kind of funny because I could see him, but I couldn't see you." A look of revulsion crossed Mule's face.

"What's wrong?" I asked.

She replied, "I saw Luther without his robe on, and he was so ugly. He was about five feet tall—my height—just ugly beyond imagination."

I said, "Describe him as best you can."

Mule said, "Well, he mostly looked like a skeleton with some patches of white, wrinkly skin. The skeleton was outlined with an orange glow, like a halo of fire. He didn't have any eyes, just sockets where the eyes were supposed to be. His hands were really ugly too. The fingers were long and bony with twisted nails."

Mule began to cry softly at the horror that words could not adequately convey.

I said, "It's okay, Mule. Jesus was helping us, and he will continue to do so."

Mule managed a smile and said, "I know Jesus was helping."

"How do you know that?" I said.

Mule said, "Luther was very mad at you, but he was real scared at the power that was coming through you. Then, I heard a voice tell Luther to quit hiding behind the robe and to reveal himself to me as he really was. It was definitely not your voice, so something just told me it was Jesus."

With a look of wonder, Mule added, "I guess he really does exist, doesn't he?"

"As I have said," I said.

Mule asked, "Will Luther come back?"

"I don't think so," I said. "I told him to go away in the name of Jesus, so I don't think he can bother you anymore."

It was the reply of a novice.

Later that evening, as I lay in bed, I reflected upon the battle with Luther. In my wildest imaginations, I had never expected to be in the position of casting a demon out of a human being. Now, I had actually made intercession for Mule against the demon that had been tormenting her so viciously. And Jesus himself had helped us.

In a sinking instant, I sensed the presence of overwhelming evil. The sound of crackling flames began to build until the volume almost convinced me the house was on fire. The smell of something like burning flesh filled my nostrils. I leaped out of bed and searched for the cross that I had been given upon my confirmation to the church.

Be it known that intercession often prompts revenge.

Chapter 9

Wait On the Lord and Be of Good Courage

June 16, 1984

Luther was still around; we had battled numerous times over the previous two weeks. Today's battle had been particularly grueling. Yet that was not my concern.

A full five minutes had passed since I had dispatched Luther, yet the part of Mule that he displaced when he possessed her (known as the essence of her soul) had not yet returned to her earthly body. Mule was lying limp before me; for practical purposes, an empty shell. Yet her head was cocked attentively, as though listening to an important message.

Mule found herself standing beside Heaven's lake. Yet in contrast to Luther's deceptive vision, this was reality. Directly overhead, a low-flying, billowy, white cloud hovered over the lake's edge.

From behind the cloud, Jesus spoke, "I love you very much. You are good, but to see me, you must first believe in me. You can come to the lake to stay, but you will have to wait until it is time." Jesus then dispatched the essence of Mule's soul back to her earthly body.

I was greatly relieved when Mule returned. She opened her eyes and began crying.

"What's wrong, Mule?" I asked.

She said, "I don't want it all to be a dream, because then there will be nothing that I know. If I love Jesus, will he go away like everybody else?"

"What are you talking about, Mule?"

Mule said, "Jesus talked to me from behind a cloud. He told me that he loved me, and that I could go to Heaven to stay when it was time. He seemed very concerned about me, but knowledgeable about how everything will turn out. He didn't have an accent I could place, but it's a real nice voice."

"I would suspect so," I said in wonderment. "I would suspect so."

June 30, 1984

Mule was hypnotized by the streaming fingers of sunshine that filtered through her living room blinds. She watched with fascination as the light took on an unnatural, reddish cast. "How strange," Mule thought. As the diffuse light beams evolved into a fiery hue that traced the outline of a distorted figure, a familiar terror gripped Mule. She stared helplessly as Luther took full form from the reddish light. He now appeared just as he truly was, never again to be hidden behind the facade of the monk's robe.

With a gruesome grin, Luther waved his hand in sarcastic greeting. "Hello, my dear," he rasped.

Mule froze in fear as she watched Luther's eyeless sockets gush gallons of blood that pooled at his feet. He sneered, "Do I have your attention now, my dear?"

Luther shrieked at Mule, "I'm very angry with you for trying to get more help! I know the wicked man has now found a priest to help him. I tried my best to prevent it though."

Mule asked, "Where have you been?"

Luther replied, "Sometimes I am home, and sometimes I am not. I come and go as I please. I am not chained to my possessions. You had better keep quiet and mind your own business so this goes no further. Then no one will be certain that I am still here. That is our secret. Forget that I exist, and it will go easier for you."

"Why do you bother me?" Mule asked. "Why *me*?"

Luther said, "I came to you as a voice when you were just in kindergarten. No one gave you any attention, and I was the only one who would play with you. You needed a demon because you were lonely and needed someone."

Mule said, "But now I have Jesus."

Luther shook his head. "You need me because Jesus is way too busy to ask him to be your friend. Believe me, no one would be as honest with you as I am. I'm warning you, though, not to get involved with the church. I have no authority in the church."

Mule said, "I never know for certain when you are here."

"Yes, I know," Luther replied with great pride. "That's one of the joyous things about owning a human. We make you do things you despise and then leave you holding the bag. As long as humans don't believe we exist, we have free rein."

With a defiance born of growing strength, Mule said, "Well, you can't play with me anymore. I won't let you."

Luther snarled, "How foolish, my dear. I can possess you anytime I wish."

Mule said, "But now I am a Christian. I believe in Jesus, so you have to go away."

Luther asked, "Then why am I still here after the wicked man told me to go away in the name of Jesus?"

Mule had no answer.

Luther explained: "My dear, the issue is not whether or not you believe in Jesus. Even evil spirits believe in Jesus in that sense, because we see he exists. But that's not the point. The point is how much Holy Spirit you have, and you barely have a seed. You are filled with darkness."

Mule protested, "But Farmer said that as long as I believe in Jesus, you have to go when I tell you."

Luther spat, "The wicked man is a fool. A poison brier can easily choke a mustard seed."

"The process," Luther continued, "is so simple. The absence of God leads to temptation; temptation leads to human sin; human sin results in greater darkness within your soul; the more darkness, the better home you make; and the better home you make, the more desirable it is to possess it. And I possess you. You belong to me."

The enraged Luther lusted for blood. "Enough foolishness, my dear. It is time to call the wicked man to come over. Then, I want you to hide behind the door and stab him when he walks in. Don't worry, with my strength behind you, it will be a cinch."

Mule said, "But I don't want to kill him. He's been trying to help me."

Luther said, "Why not kill him? That man is eager to get to Heaven. He has no fear of death. And while he is bleeding to death, you can kill yourself by taking all your pills. Then you will get to go to Heaven too. See? That will work out best for all concerned. To die together is a very loving thing."

Mule crumpled to the ground, totally helpless before the evil onslaught.

July 2, 1984

At night's zenith, Mule obediently got out of her bed, walked to the kitchen, and retrieved Luther's favorite carving knife from the cutlery drawer. Holding the knife at arm's length, she prepared to plunge the blade deep into her stomach. She was dimly aware of what she was doing, but it caused her no alarm. Luther had taken away her fear.

Mule took a deep breath and started to strike. Yet an unseen force restrained her arm. She tried again—but again her arm was restrained. As contradictory impulses of life and death waged a furious struggle within her soul, she could only gaze at the knife with morbid fascination. Finally, she slumped down from fatigue onto the cold kitchen floor.

As morning light approached, Mule distinctly heard a gentle, sweet female voice. The words sounded unusual, almost archaic, but they comforted Mule beyond understanding.

The voice spoke, "Wait on the Lord and be of good courage."

July 3, 1984

In the morning, Mule had seen a Catholic priest who was at least willing to consider the possibility that she might have demon problems. The priest had suggested that she acquire a crucifix and pray, "Jesus, mercy," whenever she was under demon attack.

Now, as she lay in bed at day's end, she held her crucifix and tenderly stroked Jesus' wounds, trying to imagine how much pain he had endured on the cross.

Suddenly, the bedroom lights flashed off, and Mule's crucifix was snatched from her hand. After a dramatic pause for effect, Luther spoke in his familiar raspy whisper: "The wicked man is lying to you. I'm not ever going to let you be free from me."

Then, to Mule's horror, Luther's gaunt face transformed into a perfect likeness of her earthly father's face. In the exact voice of Mule's earthly father, Luther said, "Daddy caught you out of bed, and now you are going to be in big trouble." Mule understood at this moment that Luther had sometimes influenced her father to harshly discipline her.

Luther then mimicked the face and voice of Mule's mother: "Be a good little girl and take all of your medicine."

In his own voice, Luther added, "You see, my dear, I have more influence than you could possibly imagine. I can always get to you by going through others. There are lots of Judases out there. Do you really think it's possible for you to be free from me?"

Luther was eager to punish Mule for her continuing rebellion. But mercifully, the bedroom lights flashed back on, and the sinister spirit disappeared with the shadows.

Mule again heard the unknown female voice speak, "Wait on the Lord and be of good courage."

Chapter 10

The Regression

July 4, 1984 (day)

An ominous feeling gripped me. Unless there was trouble, Mule would have made her usual check-in call. I called her to investigate. After many rings, the phone was lifted from the receiver, but no one spoke.

"Mule, is that you?" I inquired.

After a very long silence, Mule asked in the voice of a timid, preschool child, "Who are you?"

I said, "Don't be silly; you know who this is. Why didn't you call me at the appointed time?"

"Do I know you?" she asked with true innocence.

I had no time for foolishness. "Mule, quit playing games. Why are you talking like a little girl and acting silly?"

Then it came to me—Luther had struck again. But what had he done to Mule?

I warily asked, "Mule, how old are you?"

She proudly replied, "I can count it on my hand."

"That's good," I said. "Go ahead."

She counted slowly and deliberately: "One, two, three, four."

I said, "So you are four years old, Mule?"

"I'm so big," Mule said proudly.

What was I to do now? Luther had possessed Mule and regressed her into a fully grown woman with the mind of a four-year-old child. Danger!

"Mule," I said, "do you know who Jesus is?"

"Oh, yes, I know who he is," she replied sweetly. "He is the one who makes the birds sing for you."

I said, "He makes the birds sing for you?"

Mule said, "Yes, when your ears hurt and you can't hear, he makes the birds sing for you so you won't be all alone."

"Yes, Mule," I congratulated, "that's right. Can you say Jesus' name for me?"

Mule said, "That's a very hard word to say."

I said, "Yes, it is. Can you spell Jesus?"

"Oh, that is spelled very funny," she said. Luther was trying his best to prevent Mule from calling on Jesus.

I urged, "Show me you are a big girl, Mule, and try to spell Jesus for me."

Mule said, "I am smart. Did you know that if you put an *o* at the end of God, it spells good?"

"Yes, that is very smart, Mule," I said. It was time to try another route. "Mule, I want you to look at yourself in the mirror, because I think you might be older than four."

Suddenly stricken with terror, Mule said, "I can't look at myself in the mirror."

"Why not?"

Mule said, "Because nothing will be there. Luther says that I am nothing without him."

To know Luther was to despise him. I said, "Mule, Luther is wrong to hurt you. Jesus loves you, and he would never hurt you."

Mule said, "I have been playing with Luther this morning, but don't you tell anyone. Luther said he was going to bring some friends over to play, but not to tell the wicked man. Oh, no. Are you the wicked man?"

I said, "It's okay to tell me anything, Mule. What have you been playing with Luther?"

She said, "Luther likes to play jump rope, and do you know what? Even when he doesn't jump, the rope goes right through him. But it hits my feet and makes me fall. It hurts."

I had enough of Luther. I said, "Mule, tell Luther that I think he must be a most brave and powerful being to be able to play with your little spirit. Ask him if he would like to play with mine?"

Mule began to panic. She said, "I have to get off the phone right now. Daddy doesn't like for me to be on the phone when he's not home."

I said, "I would like to bring Jesus and come over and play too. Can we come over and play too?"

Mule said, "I can't reach the doorknob to let you in. It's too high."

I said, "But we want to play too."

Mule scolded, "Now if you bring over too many friends, daddy will be mad."

I said, "But Jesus wants to visit with you. He loves you."

With great sadness, Mule replied, "Nobody loves me."

She quickly changed the subject. "Do you want to share a snack with me?"

"What snack?" I sighed. I had no idea where this excursion would lead.

Mule said, "You can share my apple. Let me cut some for you?"

"Mule, you don't have a knife do you?"

Mule said, "Yes, because Luther was teaching me how to cut the apple when you called. But he said before I cut the apple, I have to cut my fingers off."

I gasped. "Don't do it, Mule."

"You see," Mule explained, "Luther plays with me by hurting me, and I have to let him or he will go away, and then I will be all alone."

I was learning more about Luther than I could stomach. I said, "It's okay to let Luther go away, Mule. You can get better friends."

Mule admonished me: "But Luther says he is my best friend, and I have to believe him or he will hurt me. He said this was the best game ever. He said it was great fun to fool everyone into thinking he might be gone."

I wanted to get my hands on Luther's throat, but I was more than fifteen minutes journey away. I said, "Mule, Luther is not very nice."

Mule huffed, "You are very wrong. He's my friend. And did you know that his father was a prince, just like in the fairy tale books? That's special, huh?"

"He's not a prince anymore," I replied. "He fell."

Mule didn't understand the abstraction. "Luther likes to fall off of high places too. He said it was fun to fall, and you wouldn't hurt afterwards. Luther told me that everything was just in my head anyway, and I don't know whether anything is real or not. He said we make a great pair."

The conversation continued in this vein for many more minutes. Eventually, with much prompting, Mule was able to call on Jesus. Luther's hold was then broken, and Mule recovered her adult faculties. She had no recollection of what had just transpired.

I called the Catholic priest and made an appointment for the next day. The priest said that he planned to recite a special prayer for Mule. He supplied no further details, and I asked for none.

As I reviewed my notes, I took some time to consider Mule's statement, "Jesus makes the birds sing."

When Mule was three years old, she had endured an ear infection that had left her nearly deaf. This condition, coupled with the psychological and spiritual instability of her family, had resulted in an austere emotional isolation.

To pass the lonely hours between her ear operations, Mule would often stare out her bedroom window and watch the birds that perched on a nearby tree. She would strain to hear their chirping, for in her mind, this would herald an improvement in her condition. Usually, she heard nothing—nothing at all.

Yet at times of wonder, the sounds of the singing birds would pierce the silence in a most glorious way. And in that magical economy of feeling and expression that children have by nature, Mule had captured the essence of theological understanding: "Jesus makes the birds sing."

It had been her only source of hope, before hope had become just a memory.

Chapter 11

Pretty Angel

July 4, 1984 (evening)

I was keeping an overnight watch on Mule because I suspected Luther would try to interfere with her scheduled meeting with the Catholic priest in the morning. My suspicions were correct.

I commanded, "Luther, in the name of Jesus, quit your endless deceptions and confront me."

An ever-so-slight smirk came across Mule's lips. It was Luther. He knew that I knew, but he mockingly played possum.

I instinctively reached for a nearby crucifix and pressed it against Mule's forehead. Luther scowled and began a slow squirm.

"Let's try again, Luther," I said. "In the name of Jesus, leave her alone and confront me."

Luther's evil spirit surged forth. He slung the crucifix off his (Mule's) face with a guttural growl. "She is mine, wicked man. She belongs to me."

I countered, "She belongs to Jesus."

Luther was incensed at my opposition to his claims. His strength had been increasing over the days, as other evil spirits no doubt reinforced him. Finally, after much struggle and prayer, I expelled Luther, and Mule's body went limp.

Mule moaned, "It's hot, hot, hot, dark, dark, dark." She pleaded, "Help me, please."

Though Luther had left the container of Mule's body, the essence of her soul had not yet returned. There was nothing to do for her now except to pray.

After several minutes, the breathless Mule reached her hand out and grabbed for something unseen to my eyes. "Pretty angel," she sighed, "pretty angel."

The last thing Mule remembered, Farmer had been mumbling something about demons. She didn't know why, but she was both angry and scared of him. She wanted to kill him. Then Farmer had gone berserk and pressed a crucifix—a hot one at that—right onto her forehead. This ejected her out of her body and into the realms of darkness.

To Mule's utter dismay, she now found herself trapped in the deeper layers of Hell, quite close to the core. Although the furnace blast of the core's fires rose to toast her, there was no accompanying light. Hell was so black that she could not even see her upraised hand in front of her face. The air's stench left her in the throes of a continual gag reflex. Yet despite her fervent wish to lose consciousness, she remained quite alert and aware of her torment.

Luther left his confrontation with Farmer and stood before Mule. With a flamboyant wave of his hand, concentric circles of lighted candles appeared and surrounded them in tiers.

Luther positioned his face inches from Mule's. He rasped, "Since you like going to churches so much, how do you like my church? You won't be going to any other, my dear."

Luther pulled back, pointed to the surrounding candles, and hissed, "My power comes from the fire. The true light of the world is my father."

Mule was beyond scared. She heard the frenzied screams of condemned souls piercing the darkness.

Luther laughed and then said, "I don't like the cross you got from the wicked man. Obviously, it is just a piece of metal. You see, Jesus doesn't make it down here very often."

The voice of Jesus then rang out from Heaven: "Go help her and be very gentle."

Luther cowered at the sound of Jesus' voice. He looked up, saw a shaft of light bearing down upon him, and made a hasty retreat.

Mule watched the light descend and surround her, forming a protective cocoon as a shield against the darkness. Out of the light, a gentle, familiar female voice spoke, "Wait on the Lord and be of good courage."

As Mule stared in reverent wonder, the light formed into the shape of an unbelievably beautiful female with wings. "Pretty angel," Mule cried out as she reached for the angel's outstretched hand, "Pretty angel."

The holy angel, with penetrating eyes of azure blue, smiled down at Mule, grasped her hand, and said, "I am your angel; Jesus sent me."

The holy angel, clothed in humble grace, was far more beautiful than the most beautiful of earthly women. She had long golden-blonde hair that cascaded down the shoulders of her simple robe of purest white. A shimmering halo of light traced her entire outline, not merely her head. The angel not only radiated light, she was of the light, dazzling and glorious.

Mule took a quick peek at the wings attached to the angel's back and noted that they were not at all like a bird's wings.

The translucent wings were delicately crafted, not pointy with feathers, but more rounded and full with smooth lines.

The angel was amused that her wings had drawn Mule's curiosity. She laughed gently, looked into Mule's eyes, and again said, "Wait on the Lord and be of good courage." In the next instant, the essence of Mule's soul was returned to her earthly body.

Mule opened her eyes, looked at me, and exclaimed, "The angel was so pretty!"

"You actually saw an angel?" I said.

Mule said, "Yes, but one thing puzzles me. Why did Jesus send the angel to get me instead of coming himself?"

I could only smile at the innocence of such a question. Mule had quickly progressed from believing that Jesus was a fairy tale to expressing slight dismay that he had not personally chauffeured her from Hell.

Chapter 12

I Know All About Luther

July 5, 1984

Mule shook with wild-eyed panic as we awaited the arrival of the Catholic priest in the church sanctuary. "What is Holy Water?" she said. "Luther just said that Holy Water would burn me. Please don't let any Holy Water get on me."

I had no prior knowledge of the priest's intentions, but evidently, Luther did.

Mule's eyes rapidly scanned the church. She pointed to a window that opened to an adjacent courtyard and blurted: "There's Luther. He is motioning for me to come outside."

Mule tried to bolt from the pew. I grabbed her in a bear hug and held on. She placed her fist squarely in the middle of my chest and pushed as hard as she could to escape.

I said, "It is okay, Mule. You are safe. Luther can't come in here, or he wouldn't be outside."

The priest entered the sanctuary dressed in his sacramental robes and cast a wary eye at the turmoil in the front pew; yet dutifully, he asked no questions and began to recite his prayers. After he finished, he reached behind the nearby lectern and retrieved a silver goblet filled with Holy Water.

Mule's screams echoed in the otherwise silent church, "Don't let him do it! Please, don't let him do it!" She struggled frantically to break my hold.

The priest approached the front pew, moistened his fingers with Holy Water, and traced the outline of the cross on Mule's forehead. Mule then began a loud, uninterrupted wail that continued longer than a human being could possibly have breath for. When she was out of air, she collapsed into my arms, totally spent. The priest watched with empathetic silence as I carried Mule away.

I drove Mule home and placed her on the sofa. She immediately curled up and fell asleep. Within a few minutes, her lips began moving as though she were talking with someone.

———

The angel who had retrieved the essence of Mule's soul from Hell the previous day spoke, "My name is Katrina, and Jesus would like to speak with you now."

Katrina grasped Mule's hand and instantly transported the essence of her soul to the lake in Heaven. Mule and Katrina held hands and gazed at the cloud overhead.

From behind the cloud, Jesus spoke, "Sending Katrina does not mean I'm not there; I'm always there. I thought you needed to see someone, and it is not time for you to see me yet. But I have given you a lot of people to help you."

Jesus' voice then became quite stern: "I know all about Luther; Luther is going to lose the game."

Returning to his usual gentle tone, Jesus continued, "You have to go through all of this, not because I'm punishing you, but to make you stronger. There's a lesson in it that you will find out about later. Luther will have to come back a few more times, but the stronger you both get, the less he will come. I've given you the strength to resist Luther, but I won't make him go away just like that, because then you wouldn't know how much you need me."

Mule could not contain her joy in Jesus' presence and said, "The angel is so pretty."

Jesus said, "All things in Heaven are beautiful."

Jesus continued, "I love all my children, but they all need to learn, so I won't do everything for them. Remember: I'm not punishing you; I'm strengthening you. I'm always there and always will be there, no matter how afraid you get."

Mule said, "Teach me to love you."

Jesus said, "In time. Listen to everything Farmer tells you, because I'm working through him. I'm helping him to know you better, and I'm also working to make him stronger and to prepare him. Farmer has his own angel, and she knows to look out for him. She was sent to earth to help strengthen him."

Mule said, "When can I actually see you?"

Jesus said, "You'll see me when the time is right, but always remember to wait on the Lord and be of good courage. I love you very much, and later on you will both understand."

Jesus' voice then filled with majesty and he proclaimed, "I've given you many good things inside so…"

Then, Jesus paused. Mule and Katrina continued to look upward while waiting for Jesus to speak again. Jesus said nothing. Was Jesus still behind the cloud? Had he been called away?

Mule looked at Katrina and asked, "What happened to Jesus?"

Katrina continued to stare at the cloud.

Mule again asked Katrina, "Where's Jesus?"

Katrina bit her lip hard to stifle a laugh. Mule looked back up to the cloud.

Jesus waited for just the right moment and finished his sentence: "…so loosen up a little, will you?"

Mule did not know how to interpret Jesus' meaning. She looked over at Katrina who broke into a gentle laugh. Finally, Mule got the joke and laughed too.

Be it known there is great humor in love.

———

Mule's sudden laugh startled me. She opened her eyes and said, "He's funny. He told me to loosen up a little. I didn't expect him to talk like that."

"Who, Mule?" I said.

"Jesus," she replied.

I wondered whether the adoration upon her face matched the astonishment in mine.

Chapter 13

Follow My Name

July 7, 1984 (day)

Katrina appeared to Mule on earth and said, "Come for a few moments." Katrina then escorted the essence of Mule's soul to the lake in Heaven, where again, the single white cloud hovered above the calm waters.

And Jesus spoke from behind the cloud: "Rest, my child, for there are but two battles to come. You will need your strength to fight. Be assured the battle is won, but remember to wait on the Lord and be of good courage. Remember also to reach out to the one who helps you, for when it is done, you will both know the lesson."

Katrina then returned the essence of Mule's soul to her earthly body.

Mule called me and relayed Jesus' message. She asked, "What does it mean?"

I said, "It means that Luther is in big trouble. Rest, like Jesus told you, and I will be over as soon as possible." I then hung up the phone and prepared to depart.

Mule called again and said, "I just heard a voice that I've never heard before. It was a male voice, but it definitely wasn't Jesus. He said to 'prepare a Communion.' What's a Communion?"

I said, "I will explain later, Mule. First, ask the voice whether we should go to a church to do this."

Mule asked the question and received a response: "When two or more are gathered, there is a temple."

As long as Mule was receiving direct answers to direct questions, I thought I would have her ask another one: "Ask him what the Communion is for."

The male voice returned to Mule, "Communion is to receive strength in times of trial: when shared, all are strengthened in the Lord and of each other. Thus it is said of twice done."

The words were spoken in a distinctive style that would become quite familiar to me over time. But for now, I could only conclude that the voice did not belong to a demon.

I had one remaining question for Mule to ask the male voice: "Should I give the Communion?"

He replied to Mule, "Tell him yes."

Mule fought nobly to resist the waves of fatigue that washed over her.

I said, "Go ahead and go to sleep, Mule. It doesn't matter to Luther. He can come whether you are asleep or awake."

Mule said, "Maybe if I am awake, I can fight better."

I said, "It's okay to try to stay awake if you want to, but I think sleep is more important. Right now, Luther's spirit is stronger than yours, so I will stand up for you. When you get stronger, I'll turn you loose, tiger."

Mule said, "I'm still going to try to stay awake."

"Suit yourself," I said. Three seconds later she was asleep.

I closely observed Mule's movements and facial expressions, ready to pounce at the first hint of Luther's arrival. If Luther could sneak into Mule's temple without my notice, he could roost unhindered. My task was to catch his first move. For, as usual, the quicker the detection, the faster the eviction.

After a long period of monitoring the sleeping Mule, I went to retrieve a glass of water. When I returned, I stood next to the sofa and saw her body give a slight lurch. A familiar uneasiness descended upon me. With eyelids closed, Mule's head turned upward and looked me in the eye. This meant trouble.

I traced the outline of the cross on Mule's forehead and said, "Luther, in the name of Jesus, I command you to make yourself known to me."

Luther, wearing a malevolent mask of evil, quickly came forth in full power. "Hello, wicked man. Want to play?"

Before I could react, Luther's fingernails raked Mule's arms, leaving nasty scratches etched in her flesh. This explained the marks that had drawn my attention months earlier.

Luther (in the container of Mule's body) scrambled off the sofa and tried to bully his way past me. I blocked him backwards onto the floor, straddled him, and pinned his arms over his head. As he struggled against my hold, I noticed his strength had again increased from earlier battles. It took all my effort and body weight to leverage his arms downward.

I spoke sternly, "Luther, in the name of Jesus, I command you to release her and depart."

Luther hissed, "She's mine, wicked man. My father told me that I could have her to play with as long as I wanted."

I said, "She belongs to Jesus."

"No, no, no, no," Luther droned on monotonously. "You don't play fair, wicked man."

Luther's strength tired me to the point where I did not know whether or not I could continue to restrain him. He noticed my difficulties and began to struggle even harder, desiring to overwhelm me. While I was preoccupied with his flailing arms and torso, his legs were free. With an inspired grin, he began to rhythmically knee me in the back, as though keeping time for a marching band.

As I winced from the force of the blows, Luther mocked the Communion that Mule and I had taken: "You see, wicked man, bread doesn't give strength."

After another half hour of intense struggle, Luther finally weakened. "Luther, be gone in the name of Jesus," I said breathlessly.

Luther conceded: "I'll be back, wicked man, but next time it might not be so easy. I'm going to bring even more friends to play next time."

Mule's panicked voice faded in: "Where am I? How do I get back?" she asked. Though Luther had departed, the essence of Mule's soul had not yet returned to her body.

Mule muttered excitedly, "Follow name, follow name." I had no idea what she was referring to. "Follow name, follow name," she repeated, a bit more loudly each time. Finally, the essence of her soul returned and quickened her body.

I said, "What happened to you, Mule?"

Mule said, "I was sleeping, and Luther came and took me away to that same hot, dark place and left me there. He said that my friend wanted to play, and he just couldn't wait. Did he play with you?"

I said, "Yes, Mule, we had a good game. By the way, how did you get back?"

Mule said, "Well, I couldn't find my way out of the darkness. I was completely lost. Then, I heard Jesus calling to me."

"What did he say, Mule?"

"Jesus said, 'Follow my name.'"

Chapter 14

Luther Loses the Game

July 7, 1984 (evening)

If Luther was, indeed, going to retrieve more demonic reinforcements, I thought it best to seek assistance. Miriam bravely consented to aid me in restraining Luther during his final attack.

Around 9:00 p.m., Mule said, "I just heard a voice say, 'Anointeth thy head with oil.' It was the same voice that said to prepare a Communion."

We searched and found some olive oil that Mule had purchased for an untried recipe. Since I had no experience with anointing, I went on instinct. I asked for God's blessing on the oil and sprinkled some on top of all three of our heads.

Mule grabbed the oil from me and said, "No, like this." She then dipped her fingers into the oil and traced the outline of the cross onto our foreheads. There could be no doubt that this lamb of little understanding was being guided in her actions.

Mule then heard the unknown male's voice say, "Read the first part of Psalm 35 and believe."

After we read the psalm, Mule nervously asked her guiding voice, "What should we do now?"

"Wait on the Lord and be of good courage," he replied. "Don't worry: the Lord is standing near with his armor."

Mule, Miriam, and I then partook of Holy Communion as instructed. Afterwards, I tucked Mule into her temporary sleeping quarters on the sofa and took up a nearby position for observation.

I said, "Mule, I want you to sleep if you can, but first, ask the voice if you should hold on to your crucifix. You've scraped your arms several times with it during the battles with Luther."

The voice that answered was clearly Katrina's: "Hold on to Jesus as long as you can, but the commands of the Lord are radiant. Don't worry, for there are many other blessed ones (holy angels) to help."

I watched Mule carefully as she slept with her crucifix lightly clutched in her hand. Around midnight, almost imperceptibly, she began to alternately grasp and release the crucifix. As time went on, the intensity of movement increased. Luther was trying to gain ascendancy, yet Mule was gamely resisting him.

The spiritual struggle played itself out in the physical realm: When Mule's hand squeezed the crucifix, a scowl of contempt etched onto Luther's countenance; when her grip loosened, an evil grin twisted his lips. At times, I would help Mule hold the crucifix by squeezing her hand shut, prompting low, guttural growls from Luther.

As the struggle progressed, Mule's hand made fewer autonomous attempts to hold on to the crucifix. Her resistance wavered, and her body gradually went limp. Luther had temporarily subdued Mule, yet he was not fully present to be confronted.

Mule's face, now a reproduction of Luther's, displayed a range of emotions unrelated to what was happening on earth. He frowned, he laughed, he snarled—but it had nothing to do with anything I was aware of. His fingertips tapped against his chin, as though pondering a perplexing problem. He tracked an unknown target back and forth. One of his feet pawed at the sofa, like a bull making ready to charge the toreador.

I had to retrieve Mule. "Luther, in the name of Jesus, I command you to leave her alone and confront me."

Luther's spirit suddenly filled Mule to overflowing. A sickening, sulfuric smell (burning flesh came to mind) engulfed the room—the smell of Hell.

Luther struggled to his feet from the sofa and propelled Mule's body towards the door to escape. I knocked him backwards onto the floor and sat upon his torso, while Miriam wrapped both of her arms around his legs. Luther thrashed Mule's body against the floor, as though no skeletal bones could contain him. He levitated slightly, despite the weight of my body and Miriam's pressing him downward. The enraged Luther was a frenzy of evil.

"Hate, hate, hate," Luther chanted mindlessly. "I hate her, and I hate you, wicked man."

Miriam was being tossed about like a facial tissue in a windstorm as she desperately tried to prevent Luther's knees from striking me in the back. Chilling sound effects added to the madness.

I commanded, "Luther, tell me by what right do you possess this woman?"

Luther puffed up and blasted a defiant wail, "*Sheeeeee's miiiii toyeeeeee*. You can't take her away from me."

"She's your *what*, demon?"

Luther said, "She's my toy. My father gave her to me a long time ago to play with. I can do anything I want with her. It's like a game."

I was enraged. "Jesus said your time was coming to an end, Luther."

"Oh, no, no, no, no," he mocked my warning.

As Miriam and I continued to do our best to dispatch Luther, I could only wonder what trials Mule was enduring.

———

Mule found herself in the hot, dark regions of Hell. To make matters worse, she had company. Approximately one dozen demons, led by Luther, surrounded her with malicious intent. They came in all sizes and shapes, but evil was their common denominator. In all of Mule's tormented life, she had never felt so far away from goodness.

"How do you like my toy?" Luther asked his evil playmates.

The demons hooted with glee at Mule's predicament. "We really like her Luther. She will be great fun to play with."

Luther said, "Oh, by the way, the wicked man will call for me soon, and I must go play with him. Satan has given me great power so I can teach him a lesson. Just amuse yourselves by playing with her when I am called away." The demons then began a slow advance towards the terrified, defenseless Mule.

Suddenly, a shining cross, standing approximately five feet tall, appeared out of Hell's darkness. The demons, momentarily stunned by the sight, lost track of Mule. She took the opportunity to dash for the beacon of hope. She grasped on to the cross with all of her heart, with all of her mind, with all of her soul, and with all of her strength.

Now the demons had a problem: how could they lure Mule from the safety of the cross? They could not approach Mule directly because the light from the cross was painfully blinding to them. They withdrew a suitable distance. As Luther conferred with his fiendish friends on strategy, his fingertips absentmindedly tapped his chin.

Luther urged Mule, "Let go of the cross. We won't hurt you." She wisely refused.

The demons then hurled a host of insults and deceptions to lure Mule from the cross; yet she held tight.

The demons then formed a circle around Mule, joined hands, and skipped slowly in a counterclockwise direction. Suddenly, they stopped, crouched down on all fours, and pawed the ground like bulls about to charge. In unison, they shouted and hurled themselves toward Mule, but the power of the cross repelled them. They fell back, regrouped, and debated their next move.

Mule looked out onto the demons as the searing flames of Hell's core bellowed around her. She felt as scared and abandoned as she had ever felt in her life. If the demons were successful in prying her from the cross, she believed she would have to remain with them forever.

Mule resolved to stand her ground with the cross as her shield and anchor. She had never acknowledged evil's claim to her life. Live or die, she never would. She had made her choice for Jesus, and with this choice, she would stand or fall. Though she did not fully understand why it all had to be this way, she would wait on the Lord and be of good courage.

When Jesus beheld Mule's faith and courage, he was greatly pleased.

Jesus spoke to Farmer's guardian angel, "Lucinda, go and help Katrina with Mule, and I will help Farmer with Luther myself." Lucinda's arms immediately released her charge (unseen to his eyes, she had been sheltering him), and she was obedient to Jesus' command.

Jesus then fixed his eyes upon Luther and spoke in a stern, measured tone, "Luther, be done."

At the sound of Jesus' voice, Luther froze in fear. The other demons surrounding the cross became greatly distressed and gestured wildly amongst themselves.

Jesus then inhaled deeply and blew a great gust of breath towards Mule. Katrina and Lucinda joined hands and mounted the wind as it descended with power. The smiling angels cut the terrified Luther out from the herd of demons, latched on to his mangled limbs, and escorted him downward through a slippery, narrow chasm into the rumbling depths of Hell. Luther's fiendish friends had seen enough, and they scattered into the infernal darkness.

Like a bird caught in a snare, Luther was horrified by the fate that confronted him. He squealed his objections to the holy angels: "You can't do this to me. I'll tell my father. Let go of me, you wicked angels."

Katrina and Lucinda, unruffled by Luther's display, wrapped him in chains and stuffed him securely in a claustrophobic cell of solitude. Luther strained against his chains, but bound he remained. He screamed, but no sound could be heard. Mule rejoiced: By the Son, Luther was done.

Katrina and Lucinda returned to the cross, offered a hand to Mule, and swiftly guided her upward to the lake in Heaven. Again, the magnificent cloud hovered over the surface of the waters.

And Jesus spoke from behind the cloud: "You all followed directions well, and I'm very proud. There are many lessons to be learned and meditation will help you to find them. The biggest lesson was learned: wait on the Lord and be of good courage no matter what."

Jesus added, "Don't worry about your face (blemished from stress). Nothing is ugly in Heaven, and it is not important since the beauty is in the Spirit."

After Mule's return, I began a review of the night's events with her.

Jesus interjected, "Oh, by the way, God sends his love to you all." We were left without words for this highest of honors.

There were many lessons to be learned. Psalm 35 had proven to be prophetic. Luther had, indeed, been like chaff before the wind of the Lord's breath. His path to the pit had been dark and slippery, and his fate had fallen upon him by surprise. Luther would remain in the pit forever, never to play with God's children again.

As Jesus had foretold, Luther had lost the game.

Part IV

Satan's Revenge

(July 8, 1984 – July 23, 1984)

Satan will try to cross your path many times because he tests your belief. The more you believe, the madder he gets. But don't worry, because your belief in me will always save you.

– Jesus

Chapter 15

The Days Yet to Come

July 9, 1984

Now that Luther was sealed in the pit, surely the worst was over. Mule would need a lot of rest and care, but by God's grace, she was well on her way to spiritual and emotional freedom.

The ringing phone disturbed my meditation. I answered and Mule asked, "Who is Albert? I keep hearing the name 'Albert' over and over in my mind."

I said, "I have no idea who Albert is, but I sure hope it's not another demon."

Mule said, "I don't think so. It's the same voice that said to 'prepare a Communion.'"

I said, "What does Albert want?"

Mule said, "He gave me a message to give to you. I wrote it down, but I don't understand it."

"What is the message?" I asked.

Mule read Albert's words: "I have quenched thine thirst for me, and share unto each other by drinking the blessed water of long ago. Thus ye shall receive healing and internal peace for the days yet to come."

I said, "Mule, I think Albert must be a holy angel. But what is blessed water? Are we supposed to go to a church for blessed water?"

Albert replied directly to Mule, "Two or more a temple doth make when gathered in my name."

I said, "Mule, ask Albert what is the purpose for meeting together."

Albert replied, "Ye be gathering as a form of rejoicing and to receive great rest and strength for the days yet to come. All things are in nature: I am in ye, as ye are unto me. Go by the water and listen to the peace, and there I'll be."

I said, "Mule, ask Albert what he means by the 'days yet to come.' I thought we were all finished with the demons."

Albert said, "Wait on the Lord and be of good courage."

Mule said, "What is a sacrament?"

I said, "Why do you ask?"

Mule said, "Yesterday, the word 'sacrament' kept popping into my mind. I saw a glimpse of someone with his arm around me in the most magnificent garden. In the background, I could hear a choir singing an old church hymn: 'In the Garden,' I think, is the name. What does all this mean?"

I said, "I don't know, Mule, but I am sure we will find out."

As Mule joyously contemplated Luther's demise, she relaxed her cares away in a hot bath. Suddenly, the lights went off, and the strong smell of Hell filled the air. In a panic, Mule fumbled for the bathtub stopper in the darkness. She finally managed to dislodge it. By the deceptions of the wicked, water suctioned down the drain with whirlpool force, pulling her head underwater.

THE DAYS YET TO COME 87

A chorus of demons began to chant, "Revenge her; revenge her; revenge her." The demons laughed unmercifully as Mule flailed about the bathtub.

In desperation, Mule lifted herself and shouted, "Go away, demons—in the name of Jesus!" The demons scoffed at such a command given by so weak a spirit.

Suddenly, the lights flashed back on, and the bathwater stilled. The demon sounds halted; their vile smell wafted away.

Mule regained her equilibrium, exited the tub, and counted her blessings. But what had scared the demons away? The mystery was quickly solved.

Katrina said, "Wait on the Lord and be of good courage."

Albert added, "Fear not, for a watchful eye is upon you."

Chapter 16

Divine Comfort

July 10, 1984

In her fear and despair, Mule scolded me: "I thought you said that all the problems would be over after Luther was gone."

I said, "I'm learning as I go, just like you. We'll just keep dealing with the demons until they are all gone. Don't worry; you will make it. Jesus already said that you were going to go to Heaven someday. So no matter what the demons do, they will lose in the end."

Mule said, "All day I heard the words 'grave concern.' What does that mean?"

I said, "Sounds to me like the demons are trying to intimidate you."

Mule then looked upward and began blinking her eyes in disbelief.

"What's wrong?" I said.

Mule said, "I see Katrina and Lucinda standing beside the lake in Heaven."

Surrendering to a greater power, Mule slumped over onto her chair and became quite still.

Mule found herself standing between Katrina and Lucinda on the banks of Heaven's lake. Overhead, the familiar cloud suddenly appeared.

From behind the cloud, Jesus spoke: "I know you don't understand, but if I spelled it out, you would stop looking for me. You have to learn as you go, but I have sent the angels to watch out for you and to help you.

"I am concerned about you, as I am concerned about all my children because I love them. However, 'grave concern' is from the evil side, because they can't stand to lose to good, though they always will.

"Both of you are in good hands as always, and you are in good hands on earth with Farmer. Part of your lesson is to learn how you need people, and that is why you're not happy with the way you feel. The messages on 'sharing' concern this aspect.

"Wait on the Lord and be of good courage. No matter how hard evil fights, they'll never win. But they cannot accept it."

July 11, 1984

I was too tired to answer the ringing telephone. Telephones just brought problems. Dealing with evil on a constant basis had completely drained my energy. Yet perhaps the call was from Mule, and she had it tougher than me.

"Hello," I answered.

Mule said, "I just got a message for you from Jesus. I thought you might want to know what he said before we meet later on."

My energy increased. "Are you sure it was Jesus and not Albert?"

Mule laughed at me. "Oh, sure. Their voices are very different."

I said, "Cut me some slack. You're the one with the golden ear. So what did Jesus say?"

Mule passed along Jesus' message: "Tell Farmer my Father sends his love. He is a most obedient son."

My energy was back; bring on the demons.

———————

I watched in amazement as Mule's slow and steady emotional withdrawal evolved into a catatonic stupor, leaving her frozen in her chair, oblivious to sight, sound, and touch. Whenever she exhibited symptoms this bizarre, I knew evil was at hand. Elaborate psychological theories or medications were unnecessary. The time for confrontation was at hand.

I commanded, "Satan, in the name of Jesus, leave her alone and confront me."

Mule's eyelids immediately closed and she slumped over onto her own lap. I pushed her upright and placed my hands on either side of her head. I then lifted back her heavy-hooded eyelids with my thumbs and saw only the whites eerily staring back. I closed her eyelids and shifted my head from side to side in front of her. Mule's closed eyes closely followed my movements—utterly creepy and a prime demonic tell.

I had learned to look to the eyes, for demons hated the light, both natural and spiritual. Demons could possess Mule while her eyes were open, but not without leaving telltale signs: When Mule was possessed, her eyes would have an unnatural cast to them. She would squint when looking towards me and could not look me in the eye. Once the possessing demon was confronted, however, it would "pull down the shade" on the pupil by rolling it up out of sight. Yet the demon could still see perfectly well while hiding in the dark shadows of the soul.

I traced the outline of the cross on Mule's forehead. "Demon, I know you are here. In the name of Jesus, I command you to come forth. I further command that you feel great pain as long as you delay. Come forth."

Mule's face broke into an oily, evil grin: the characteristic smirk of demonic spirit when confronted. Her facial skin tightened and pulled backwards, giving the impression of a pointed snout. Her neck arched. Her tongue darted in and out of her mouth in a way that defied physiology. From appearances, Mule was possessed by a serpent-like demon.

I steadied the slithering, writhing Mule and said, "Demon, why do you possess this child of God? What is your mission?"

With relish, the demon said, "Revenge, revenge, revenge."

The demon squirmed with such strength that I was forced to clamp its head with a two-fisted vise grip. The demon licked and bit at my nearby hands, causing me no small discomfort in the pit of my stomach. After much struggle and delay, the demon was finally dispatched.

When Mule returned and gathered her senses, she asked, "Why does this have to continue? It's not right."

Before I could respond, she fell stone asleep on the chair.

Katrina again escorted Mule to the lake's shore in Heaven, where Lucinda and the overhead cloud met them.

From behind the cloud, Jesus spoke to Mule: "Sometimes you have to go through things you don't understand, but it's always to learn. Look around the lake; everything is there for a purpose."

Mule marveled at the harmony of the surrounding countryside. Everything had a place, and nothing was out of place. One leaf more would have been too much; one less, too little.

Mule looked upward to the cloud and Jesus said: "You have to keep looking for the nice things, because it's always worthwhile. I'm always there. Listen wisely. Do you have any questions?"

Mule did not have any questions: for in the Lord's presence, all of her questions were answered.

July 13, 1984

Mule was so confused by the multitude of demonic voices, she was not even sure there *was* a Jesus.

"No one can save you from going to Hell," a demon voice hounded her.

"How could God care about a little tramp like you?" another evil voice joined.

"The dark way, Satan's way, your way," a third voice chimed in.

Though the voices had badgered Mule for more than an hour, she had, with great fortitude, continued her work. But she was weakening. She was ready to scream with all her might to drown out the taunting sounds.

Yet suddenly, a comforting Presence surrounded her, and the evil sounds ceased. Mule gradually regained her composure. But was Jesus real? Was she going to Hell? And how did a person get to Heaven? The demons had plucked away the seeds of true understanding that had not yet taken firm root in her heart, mind, and soul.

Then Jesus replanted the priceless seeds: "Don't forget my purpose; my Father calls people to himself; you have to go to the Father through me."

Mule again understood.

Chapter 17

The Rock

July 14, 1984

I answered the phone and heard Mule's excited voice: "I've got to move the rock! I've got to move the rock! Albert said that I've got to move the rock!"

I said, "Slow down, Mule. What is the rock?" She dropped the phone and said nothing more.

I hurried over to her house, where I found her unconscious on the floor, clutching a piece of paper with some writing scrawled on it. The handwriting was Mule's; the words were Albert's.

I read: "There was once great sorrow in many hearts, for a great stone a tomb did seal: Hence what reverent glory came to all when upon the dawn it was moved and unto the world a new beginning of love and hope arose, making his word absolute. A stone may seal in sorrow and despair, but oh, how beautiful the glory that can emerge from the musty darkness when it is but set to the side.

"Your heart has been hardened over times of great trial and deeds of the Evil One. Despair not, for of Divine love can it be melted and molded to cradle abundant harvests. The stone must be rolled away to make ready for basking in the glory:

thus a rock cannot feel. There is great courage behind thy trembling heart: thus it is said of good character built from tasks and lessons sent to ye. And so it will come to pass that the rock is to be cast aside, for it seals off the path to the glorious Kingdom waiting for all God's children.

"Wait on the Lord and be of good courage, for the hurt is but only heavy with sorrow and longing, only to heal with time, love, and faith. Ye shall be aided and comforted at each push. Alas, seek ye guiding comfort from the anointed son my Father has placed great blessings upon.

"Behold, for the time is at hand. Let it begin, for many good things must be set free. The garden waits to greet thee if ye can but jar the mighty stone: for the rock blocks the light, and hence, neither in nor out can the Spirit soar. It is my wish for the task to commence. Do not fear, for abiding love surrounds thee. Move the rock. Get help now!"

I gently shook Mule to her senses (she had been under demonic attack all day as she transcribed Albert's words). I helped her to a seated position on the sofa. Her burdened torso prevented her from sitting fully upright. Mule clutched her chest and moaned, "What is wrong? I can barely breathe. It hurts."

I said, "I suppose that is the weight of the rock on your heart that Albert talked about. Try to take a deep breath."

Mule inhaled deeply, triggering sharp chest pains and violent coughing.

Albert said, "Jesus' greatest desire is to move the rock. Don't be afraid, for he will help."

Mule said, "I'm too scared to try, Albert. It hurts too much."

Albert said, "Fear not, and be less like a senseless mule."

I burst out laughing—Albert had pinned the tail on the donkey. He knew a mule when he saw one.

I asked Albert, "How do we move the rock?"

Albert said, "If there is a logjam, and there are too many logs at the mouth of the river, then the river cannot flow. Let some of the water out before flood brings ruin (Mule had to shed tears to lubricate the rock's movement)."

Mule said, "I can't cry, Albert."

Albert said, "Loosen up a bit. Maybe if you make the banks wider, the logs can get through."

Then, Jesus spoke to Mule: "Come unto me in times of trouble and in times of good—but come."

Mule groaned, "I can't move the rock. It hurts too much."

Jesus said, "Let me. Just move it a little bit. It's okay for it to hurt."

Many moments passed as Mule struggled to move the rock.

Jesus spoke to me: "You must furrow the soil to make ready the seed."

I understood that Jesus wanted me to embrace Mule in my arms. When I did so, Mule's pain slowly intensified, and she begged me to stop. Against her will, her eyes moistened. Finally, she fainted with a sigh, and the essence of her soul was whisked to Heaven.

Mule found herself in Heaven's Garden of Knowledge and Contemplation, face-to-face with Jesus, the very Son of God. Jesus looked exactly like his image on the Shroud of Turin, minus the signs of torture. No pampered King, Jesus had the rugged presence of someone well acquainted with hard work and the outdoors. His face radiated concern for Mule, but it was a happy look—like he was happy to be concerned.

Jesus wore a coarse, full-length, off-white robe with three-quarter-length sleeves. Over this robe, he wore a sleeveless sackcloth garment that hung to midthigh, which he usually wore in spiritual warfare (from whence he had just come) to dull his brilliant light. His sandals were the essence of simplicity, open toed and well worn.

Jesus took Mule's hand and spoke: "We don't have long to talk, because I know you are tired. I'm glad to see you have finally come. I've been waiting a long time. The most important thing to do was to move the rock to let me in. I know it hurts, but you don't have to move it all at once.

"You followed instructions well today. I knew if I left you alone to think about it too long, you wouldn't try to move the rock. Now it's moved a little, but there's a lot of work left to do, so don't get discouraged. The first push is the hardest, though the ones to come may seem so. I want to help you, so please ask me. You have shown great strength. Don't put off the things that hurt, because the longer you wait, the more intense they get.

"Albert is right," Jesus said, pausing momentarily for effect, "you are like a senseless mule." Jesus turned his palms upward in playful exasperation and said, "You and Carla are both so stubborn. So listen to me, will you?"

Mule pleaded, "Can I stay here with you?"

Jesus said, "No, you have a lot of work to do, but I know you are of sincere heart. Time to go back."

<hr>

"Jesus is very loving," Mule said with wonder.

I said, "Whoa, Mule, you mean you actually *saw* Jesus this time?"

Mule said, "Yes, I saw him in the Garden. You just know him when you see him. Even if you didn't believe in him, you would still know who he is at first sight."

Mule added, "By the way, who is Carla? Jesus said that Carla was as stubborn as I was."

Carla was my mother's name, something that I had never before mentioned to Mule.

<hr>

Moving the rock was now our primary task. Albert taught me how: I would stand and face Mule, embrace her, and hold her close. Then, Mule would slowly increase the depth of her breathing. The more deeply she breathed, the heavier the rock weighed upon her heart. This would eventually trigger chest pain and violent coughing. She would then break my hold and push me away in self-defense. Albert then ordered for the process to be repeated until Mule could stand no more.

As Mule progressed with her rock-moving, she began to cough up thick, blackish sputum, the likes of which I had never seen before. It seemed impossible for such a poisonous-looking substance to reside within a living person. Albert informed us that it was residue from the rock.

Mule complained to Albert, "It hurts to move the rock."

Albert said, "A heart that melteth like wax can always be remolded, oftentimes even better than before; but one of rock is next to impossible to restructure from crumbled gravel. Of course, nothing is impossible for the Lord, but it pleases him much to mold with that like wax. For it matters not how many times a soul may think it is broken, for he should be grateful he was able to feel. And ponder not on it being melted, but be rejoiceful in believing the Lord shall make it anew, thus to add even that of a new dimension, no matter how tiny."

Albert spoke to Farmer: "Beware the roaring lion."

What a puzzling thing for Albert to say. He knew that I was quite vigilant in watching for demons, for not a day passed without some evil spirit attempting to harm Mule.

Albert added, "Be thee not forgetful, for Satan is but a jealous fool, content only to seek prey of God's children."

I could only conclude that I needed to be very careful in watching for demon attacks on Mule.

Albert again instructed Mule and me to work on moving the rock. Today, however, she was in no hurry to begin because of the pain involved. She allowed herself to be lightly embraced, but did not abandon herself to fully relax as the angel ordered. The Mule needed a push, but I was reluctant to use brute force to bring her close.

Suddenly, Mule's body surged towards me. She angrily glanced over her shoulder and said, "Stop it." But again, her body surged towards me. "Stop it," she repeated.

"What's wrong, Mule?" I said.

"Somebody is pushing me," she said. "Make them stop."

The feisty Lucinda said, "Hey, you're emotionally choked. If you would just relax a little, the spasm will cease, and the fruit will go down better."

Mule said, "But it hurts to hold close to him."

Albert said, "When you need to start a fire but have not ye any wood, it is in great appreciation you accept an armload. Alas, it may be too great a gift to hold the entire load all at once, so take ye but one stick at a time: for once the fire is kindled, it into a blaze doth turn when fed with the loving care in which the wood was bestowed upon ye with."

Mule said, "But I don't want to cry. It's not right."

Albert said: "Just as the Great One died to cleanse us of our sins, we may weep in assurance of being of clean hand. As a waterfall rushes over the rocks, it worries not of its course, for its control is in the palms of the Lord; thus let go and worry not of your tears, but consider them as a graced veil of joy overlaid upon thy cheeks."

Mule eventually made some painful progress in budging the rock. As her deepening breaths prompted coughing spasms, she continued to expectorate the blackish sputum. But still, no tears.

Albert said, "Be there much pride, for the rock is ajar, but a'grain. Thou be patient, for it is of a great might to move when the ground is unbroken without visions of a path. Though each push be of pain, ye may be assured of comfort for thee in Heaven and earth."

"But, Albert," Mule said, "I will never be able to move the rock. It's too big."

Albert said: "The rock is no mightier than the power it is given. Fear not, for it is sure to erode with the touch of time, as do all things exposed.

"There is a most important lesson to acknowledge in that of a seashore: though the waves may crest and crash against the shore in rhythmic succession making a melody unto themselves, they wear the rocks away in a smoothness known only in nature. Be it known the Lord blows gently on the water."

Chapter 18

Angels of Distinction

July 17, 1984

Albert spoke to Mule: "Walk together to the temple of the Lord, stand before the altar in great praise, and be thee born of water. As they gathered at the river, so shall ye both gather at the temple to profess your faith in Christ. Just as John was called upon as a witness, so shall the one who guides ye be. Be thee not concerned with the world's denominations, but be thee a congregant in the House of the Lord. Oh, how glorious, to be thee born again."

July 18, 1984

Mule said, "Albert, why can't we rest from moving the rock? I can move it later."

Albert said, "It's okay to rest, but I know ye be like a senseless mule; and if you rest too much, you won't try again."

"But I'm so tired," Mule said. "Sometimes it seems that God isn't around anymore (a statement only Mule could make while conversing with a holy angel)."

Lucinda then spoke lovingly, but forcefully, to Mule: "God is not like a pinball machine: He never stops being with you, even if your quarter runs out."

My soul smiled. Hear, O Israel: God is not like a pinball machine—hey, simple. Listen well, theologians. Ah, the voice of individuality.

For God is not only the Father of all, but of each.

July 19, 1984

I said, "Albert, is it okay for me to ask you direct questions?"

Albert said, "I am happy to answer questions, but Jesus is guiding you, and I am guiding her via Jesus."

I said, "What kind of angel are you?"

Albert said, "I be of the order of the cherubim, yet mainly I be an angel of tidings."

Albert added, "Time to work on moving the rock."

Mule said, "Do we have to, Albert? I'm tired."

Lucinda interjected: "Get up off the mat and get ready for round two. Don't be content to be an emotional cripple. Take steps."

Mule said to Albert: "Lucinda is kind of mean sometimes, don't you think?"

Albert said: "Lucinda definitely has a different style. I prefer my way, but sometimes a stubborn Mule has to be spoken to like that."

We again went through the painful (for Mule) and laborious (for both of us) process of moving the rock. We made little noticeable progress. This rock was more like a mountain.

Albert said, "Though clouds may shower for a while, oh, how they refresh the air and revive the earth: for true it is said of a calm before the storm, and true it is of a peace after. Thus how long is the storm in relation to all the rest? Not but a mere moment, my child, not but a mere moment.

"Mighty are the works, but plentiful are the blessings. Be assured you will eat at God's table; there are never too many place settings."

I said, "Albert, are you angry with me for asking you so many questions today?"

Albert said, "Ye be of a special bond, and thus I tell ye so. And be it known 'tis no anger between ones of love."

Katrina escorted the essence of Mule's soul to a place of dazzling white light on the fringes of Heaven. Multitudes of angels, in eternal flower of youth, blissfully prepared for earthly missions.

Katrina led Mule to a nearby angel and said, "This is Albert."

Albert, the Divine Bard: earnest, contemplative, lover of lyrical language. He sported curly blond hair shaped in the style of the first–century AD Romans. His eyes, a rich shade of brown, were framed with well-defined, plush eyebrows. His cheeks were rosy and full, almost chubby, but the jawline angled sharply as it tapered to meet the chin. Yet just as with all other holy angels, Albert was perfect—though quite in his own way.

Albert cradled his ever-present lyre, made with meticulous care and craftsmanship by the angel, Gossamer. Albert's delight was playing for the sick and the blind as they slept, helping to ease their earthly passage.

Mule said, "Look, Katrina, there's Lucinda."

Lucinda had an exotic look reminiscent of a Mediterranean princess. Her slightly wavy, coal-black hair was brushed straight backwards with no part and hung well below her shoulders. Prominent cheekbones provided a classic setting for her dazzling emerald-green eyes. Lucinda had a distinctive energy about her, more active and mischievous than Katrina's; yet despite their visual differences, each angel was perfect in her own God-given way.

Mule tarried with the angels, and she received much peace and strength for her soul. She would need it; there was trouble ahead.

———

I said, "Mule, slow down so I can write down the descriptions of the angels in more detail."

Albert said, "Jason requests to speak."

I said, "Who is Jason?"

Albert said, "He be an angel ye will work with in the future."

Jason spoke:

How does someone describe the gentle breeze in your hair
 or a spring rain upon one's face?
The breeze is so much more than the movement of air:
 birds rise upon its tides; the scent of flowers and grass
 are carried in a Delicate Hand.
And isn't the rain much more than falling water?
 For it is by God's compassionate hand
 that it settles peacefully upon the plants of the field.

How then can angels,
 most holy messengers of the Most High,
 be described by the limited senses of a man?
You see, an angel perceives the substance of the flower
 and not just its form or shape.
So I will describe the substance
 and leave the rest for those
 who have the wisdom and sight to see:

The first flower *(Lucinda)* is wild in the field:
 a rare and hardy breed,
  slender in form, with a long flowing mane.
Her petals reflect the rainbow, God's arch across the heavens:
 beautiful, and impossible to grasp,
  and all the while steady and strong.
In her eyes dances the spirit of creation,
  the world born anew with vitality and life.

A short distance away in this garden of rare beauty
 stands a simple and pure flower *(Katrina)*:
  Always the same whether rain or shine,
   her blond petals turn to the sun.
Smaller in stature than the surrounding buds and flowers:
 neither pretentious, nor proud;
  neither envious, nor wanting;
   always sure and faithful.

The first flower, with eyes of green,
 dancing from here to there,
  on guard for evil snares.
The second flower, with eyes of blue,
 the truth to know and see,
  always on watch for the children of lies and deceit.

And on the field goes with its beauty so rare,
 the garden of the Master and King.

Mule's unnecessary routines were driving me to distraction: she could not relax until the cap on her toothpaste was just so; she would not let me rest until I had completely explained Albert's voluminous words of knowledge in layman's language (not an easy task); she always had to know the precise number of pennies in her piggy bank. I understood that this pseudocontrol was her way of reducing anxiety, but it was still tedious to endure.

"Mule," I said, "you are so…" I searched for the correct words to use. "You are so…"

A gentle spirit possessed Mule. She raised an eyebrow and said, "Are you trying to say 'obsessive-compulsive'?"

I stared at her. "Wait a minute, Mule. How do you know anything about psychological theory? There is no way you knew that term on your own. Is that Albert in there trying to sneak one past me again?"

Albert said, " 'Tis so."

Albert joked with Mule: "Fear not for ye toothpaste, for I need not any. I know this be such an overwhelming concern of ye."

Mule said, "Albert, are you teasing me?"

Albert said, "Yea, for ye niggle over ye pennies far beyond that of which is necessary."

<hr />

The Roaring Lion bided his time. The despised woman had destroyed his child; now, she had the audacity to plan a baptism. There would be consequences. The time for revenge was at hand.

Chapter 19

The Baptism

July 20, 1984

Albert spoke of Mule's baptism, scheduled for the following day: "In good faith ye shall stand before the altar, and of that faith ye shall receive much peace. Go ye in unison to the temple, as the Lord has conferred and beatified the bliss of Heaven upon ye both, until all can gather before him in his House for eternity. Be assured that celestial angels shall escort ye there with much joy when the time arrives."

A joyful word, indeed. Yet unexpectedly, Albert sternly said, "Get thee behind me, Satan."

"What's wrong, Albert?" I said.

He said, "Be alert for the night is near."

Perhaps Albert was warning of demon problems. Yet when I checked for this possibility, Mule was clean. "What are you trying to tell me, Albert?" I said, very confused by his cryptic messages.

Albert said, "A scheming plot be in your midst."

I said, "Albert, everything seems to be fine. What is the problem that you are trying to warn me of?"

Albert said, "Satan plays with marked cards."

I was exasperated. "Yes, I know he does, Albert. So what should I do?"

Albert said, "Though there be shade under the tree, don't linger there too long."

I would have been glad to respond in whatever way I was instructed, but I could not determine what I was supposed to do. I asked, "Can you be more specific, Albert?"

He replied, "May ye rest on it."

Though Albert's words hinted strongly at potential trouble, all appeared well. Mule was clearly not being influenced by evil at the moment. Though I was uncomfortable with the situation, there seemed to be no other alternative but to continue with moving the rock.

Yet today, Mule was even more mulish than usual. She did not follow her angelic instructions and was generally being difficult. This was understandable because it was no fun to move the rock, but the work was being slowed.

Suddenly, Lucinda forcibly pushed Mule into me and held her there. Lucinda said: "Listen to me and be still. I know I'm not your favorite person, but you need to relax and it won't hurt so much. Then you can feel the weight of the rock upon your heart."

Lucinda counted off Mule's breathing: "Inhale, one, two, three; exhale, one, two, three."

Albert said, "Lucinda be of the right knowledge."

Mule began to make some progress, coughing up great quantities of the blackish sputum. I could only marvel at her great tenacity: for not only did she have to move the rock, she had to ward off numerous demon attacks.

Albert said, "Ye heart be like a rose: pretty, sweet, and oh, so gentle. But alas, if only not for the thorns, ye would be so joyful to hold."

Jesus asked Albert, "Next time a carrot I should bring?"

"Indeed, Jesus," I thought. "Next time, bring a carrot for the Mule."

As Mule prepared to go to sleep for the night, she felt a jolt of pain in her lower left abdomen. It was the worst possible timing. With all her demon problems, she could not afford to deal with physical problems too.

Mule tried everything she knew to quiet the pain, yet it persisted and grew. It was her worst attack ever. However, as she prepared to go to the hospital emergency room, the pain mysteriously ceased. She breathed a sigh of relief. She would arrange for an appointment with her physician as soon as possible.

The Roaring Lion withdrew his trident from the woman. As he well knew, vengeance was so much sweeter if meted out at the right psychological moment. The damnable woman's time had not yet come. Not quite.

July 21, 1984

As Mule and I waited silently in the peaceful chapel for the minister's arrival and the beginning of the baptismal ceremony, she stared intently at the seven-foot cross hanging over the altar.

Mule nudged me hard in the ribs. "Do you see him?" she whispered.

"See who?"

"Jesus. He is on the cross and looking down at me."

I saw nothing, but Mule's facial expression left no doubt that she did.

Finally, the minister arrived, broke Mule's trance, and performed the baptismal rites. Afterwards, we walked out of the chapel into the bright day.

I said, "Mule, you seemed unusually composed during the ceremony."

Mule said, "That's because Jesus was standing next to me with his arm around me the whole time."

I then drove Mule to her home where she immediately fell asleep on the sofa.

———

Katrina escorted the essence of Mule's soul to Heaven's Garden of Knowledge and Contemplation.

And Jesus spoke: "I was with you at the baptism, as I am with you always. I sent Albert to you because he tells important things in beautiful words, and he carries out my orders well. I know you don't understand all about the things Albert says and directs you to do, but in faith, you must both carry them out. And because of that faith, there will be great blessings.

"I know the rock is heavy. I can move it for you, but it's just like Luther: if I did it all for you, then you wouldn't know how important I am. It's real important to try to move the rock no matter how much it hurts. The lesson is to experience it so you don't build another one. When the time is right, you can be assured I'll catch it like a ball and cast it aside.

"Satan will try to cross your path many times because he tests your belief. The more you believe, the madder he gets. But don't worry, because your belief in me will always save you. Time to go back now."

———

Upon Mule's return, I asked Albert, "What will Mule's belief in Jesus save her from?"

He replied, "Satan will never know what a fool he is for trying."

Albert's words made no sense at all to me: such is the deceptiveness of the Sly One.

Chapter 20

Roaring Lion

July 21, 1984 (evening)

After a celebratory meal prepared by Miriam, Albert continued his cryptic messages: "Think about the shade tree," he said. "If a man lies under a tree, it may be the leaves change color."

I said, "Right, Albert; times do change."

Albert said, "It is nice to rest, but don't let the seasons go by unnoticed."

I said, "Everything seems okay, Albert. What are you trying to tell me?"

Albert said, "If you sit under the shade like a sheepdog does, and he is not earning his keep, look what happens to the sheep."

"Yes, Albert," I said, "that's not good for the sheep. But what are you trying to tell me? I see no danger for the sheep."

He said, "Although a tree can cast a shadow, be it only for a short time."

I was exasperated by Albert's lack of specifics. Not knowing what else to do, Mule, Miriam, and I began playing cards to pass the time.

After a while, Albert spoke in a stern voice, "It is wise to be alert, for a wise man never plays cards with Satan."

I said, "We don't want to play cards with Satan. What's wrong?"

Albert said, "A wise man need not tarry beneath the shade tree."

Mule, Miriam, and I simply stared at one another in perplexity.

A Dreadful Presence seized the opportunity and moved into the void. The room became still—dead still. For the moment, goodness did not exist, and hope was a cruel joke. Not one to rush his fun, the Dreadful Presence lingered over his prey.

Suddenly, Mule gasped, threw her cards up into the air, and jackknifed in pain. Her hands clutched her lower left abdomen. The look on her face said she expected death at any moment.

"What's wrong, Mule?" I asked.

"Something is stabbing me, and it hurts," she replied breathlessly. "It's like last night, only much worse."

I said, "Miriam, go and call the hospital and tell them we are coming in."

Mule's body began to shake in a violent, disjointed quake: As her left side pulled to the left, her right side pulled to the right; as her torso stretched upward, her legs stretched downward. Mule's soul was in a tug of war.

"Cancel the phone call, Miriam," I called out. "This must be from evil."

Albert said, "Get the crucifix." I dug the crucifix out of Mule's purse and held it firmly between her spastic fingers.

I said, "In the name of Jesus, I command you to confront me, demon." Despite repeated commands, no demon came forth.

"What's wrong with Mule, Albert?" I asked. "What demon is this?"

Through clenched teeth, Mule repeated Albert's sobering reply: "Satan."

There was nothing for Mule to do but endure the pain. After approximately twenty minutes, the angels repelled Satan's attack, and Mule's pain ceased.

Katrina escorted the essence of Mule's soul to Heaven and spoke: "You must listen to Albert's warnings. When Satan deals a dirty deck, sometimes he slips by. What you felt was a mere nothingness compared with what we were doing for you.

"Please don't give up believing. It has nothing to do with moving the rock. Satan is sly and nasty and very angry. A jealous person will try many times, and sometimes he will sneak by. Don't worry because your belief will save you. Wait on the Lord and be of good courage."

So *that* was the point of Albert's cryptic messages: Satan himself was near. Satan had been waiting for the proper moment to exact revenge for Luther's demise, and Mule's baptism was the final indignity.

Mule showed me the foot-long bruise on her lower left abdomen where Satan had struck: incredibly, it was in the shape of a lightning bolt. It was startling to realize how much the spiritual world intertwined with the physical, just as with Mule's rock.

"Katrina," I said, "you guys could have been a bit more clear about what was going on. What should we have done when Albert warned us about something, but we didn't know what he was warning us about?"

The maternal guardian answered simply and elegantly: "Pray."

July 22, 1984

Upon the dawn, Albert spoke: "The Evil Prince has great power and is of slyness like a fox. Be he a fool of much jealousy and much like a coward, for one who prowls in darkness attacks with fear of being seen. Only at dark is there danger of a wrong step.

"As one who grieves for the loss of a son to the Hands of Love, so shall he be in hunger of revenge. When one who rules as head of the house for many years is evicted against his desires and cast down below his level, be there much pity and resentment among his own. Be it of a lesser power, they may not combat the Landlord; thus to invade the house and cause much destruction brings them much pleasure.

"When the ruler of an empire himself takes up arms in hatred, much strength is called upon in defense. Be assured the Loving Ones will win, though the earth may quake. The Commander of the heavenly armies is among us. The Evil One tempted my Father three times, and thus three tries be made in hopes to destroy ye temple to get to your soul."

⸺⸰⸰⸺

As the night wore on, Mule begged Albert, "Please don't leave me tonight."

Albert said, "I shall go when I am called; it is not for me to question."

Mule said, "Do you think the angels could do more to stop Satan?"

Lucinda interjected, "I'm going to shoot you straight—we're doing the best we can."

Albert added, "Resisting Satan shows your true love for Jesus."

I said, "Albert, since angels are so peace loving, how do they feel about fighting the demons?"

Albert said, "Combat saddens us greatly, but when you consider the enemy, it makes it easier."

I said, "Is Michael the commander of the heavenly armies you mentioned earlier?"

Albert said, "Michael is with us, but Jesus is the commander."

Albert instructed us to read a series of psalms in preparation for Satan's second attack. After we finished, he spoke to Mule: "And so it is done, and I must bid you go. When the trumpet sounds, I must make ready. It is dark where I go—but bring not the lantern, for we bring the light. Our light will expose them, and hence they must flee, but not until after much struggle.

"Even though I must bid you go, my faith tells me you shall return. It is with much sadness I leave you, but with much joy I will return; and then there will be but one more try. Ye must remember: Katrina was right—it was a mere nothingness you feel. We go in knowledge, but Satan is but a sly one."

Miriam and I took up positions seated on opposite sides of Mule. We silently awaited the inevitable. After a while, Mule looked at me with wide eyes and said, "I hear the sounds of trumpets in my head."

Albert spoke to Mule: "And so, my child, I must bid you adieu, for the trumpets beckon me."

Mule said, "Don't leave me, Albert." Yet he had already departed.

We waited. Approximately ten minutes later, Satan and his forces struck against Mule in the same manner as the previous night. I did my best to comfort her, but there was little to be done. This cross was primarily Mule's to bear.

After Satan was repelled, Katrina said to Mule: "Satan charges with a spear and rides in front of everybody else. He led the fight, but said he was going to get more reinforcements.

"It helped to have extra angels tonight, because Satan was the most angry I've ever seen him. He was breathing fire from his nose, and he was green with jealousy. You were right the baptism made him angry, because it makes your union with Jesus absolute.

"What hurts Satan the most is to lose a child. Just like the three times he tempted Jesus, he will attack you three times. Albert is right about the three times, so be sure and listen to him. Albert's with Jesus right now making plans.

"It helps to pray and believe, because it helps us to do our job better. Rest because you are going to need to. There's work to be done."

July 23, 1984

Upon the dawn, Albert spoke: "All is well when the morn breaks and the dew is on the roses. I had to meet with Jesus after last eve's attack; and it took a long time, for there was much planning to do. Jesus isn't worried, but he has much loving concern.

"Strength grows from rest, so feed thyself well. Weary are the soldiers, but fearless is the army. When night befalls thee, mighty is the battle but glorious is the victory. Thus it is said of three times done.

"Evil cannot trample hallowed ground, for a Gracious Dealer catches on to crooked players. It is one thing to allude thyself to visions of grandeur, but it is quite another to carry them out; yet go about the day with great care.

"Evil and Divine on a scale do not balance, for the Divine always has the upper hand. Though they hurl great power, they still be an army of fools. Though there be strength in numbers, how silly to take up arms against the hand of Jesus.

"Cast thy burden on the Lord, for he will gird thee in thy weary, fainting hour. Think not of the weakness of your body, but of the strength binding ye soul. When the twilight of next smiles upon you, greet thee a most renewing morn.

"The Lord shall beckon ye go to the Land of the Fadeless Day, where the beloved Garden is perfect in every way. Fear not, little flock, for abounding joy shall embrace you. And be there green pastures unlike any other ye have ever seen before awaiting.

"My Father sends his love and admiration, for believers who unite for his cause receive many blessings. Rest ye mortals of great faith, and wait on the Lord and be of good courage."

Mule needed a distraction from her upcoming trials, so she sat on the sofa and watched mindless television shows. I watched her for any signs of trouble. Suddenly, her head flew backwards, and she crumpled unconscious onto the sofa. Approximately fifteen minutes later, she opened her eyes, grabbed her head like a hung over drunk, and said, "Oh, my head hurts. What happened to my head?"

Albert said: "I turned away just for a moment, and the Serpent's tail struck."

Satan's tail is no myth.

Around 3:00 a.m., Albert spoke to Mule: "I will only leave you when the trumpet blows."

Mule asked me: "What does blaspheme mean? I keep hearing the word 'blaspheme' over and over in my mind."

I said, "Blaspheme is talking against God."

Albert said: "Those who blaspheme make the Holy One angry. All should take up arms against those who blaspheme."

Satan's third attack was imminent. Miriam and I, armed to the teeth with Bibles, crucifixes, and prayer, sat on either side of Mule.

Albert said, "Hark, the trumpets beckon me; and 'tis of utmost importance to take up sword, for the time has come. I shall return."

Mule tilted her head back and forth in a queer way. "What are you doing, Mule?" I said.

Mule said, "I hear something like stampeding horses in my head. It is going back and forth and from side to side. It is swirling around."

In the next horrifying instant, Satan struck. Again, the piercing pain was savage and intense and was focused on Mule's lower left abdomen. She shook uncontrollably. The pain was more severe than the previous two nights combined.

There was nothing I could do but place my arm around Mule and witness her agony. As the intensity of her pain varied, she slipped in and out of consciousness. She muttered mindlessly: "Why Jesus let this…, make stop…, help me…" Periodically, she grabbed my arm and squeezed hard enough to stop the flow of blood.

The minutes dragged on with excruciating slowness. Satan would surely kill Mule if Jesus did not stop him soon. I looked up to Heaven in total bewilderment at the ways of God.

Finally, Jesus said, "Enough."

Mule stopped shaking, and her sharp pain dulled to a pulsing ache. She looked at me with tears in her eyes and said, "I think it is over."

Mule heard Satan's voice fading into the distance. He explained to his followers: "I can fight the angels, but I can't fight Jesus. But I've punished her well."

Mule then fainted away, but this time, with a peaceful smile. She was on her way to Heaven's Garden of Knowledge and Contemplation.

"I'm glad to see you," Jesus said as he offered his hand to Mule. She took Jesus' hand, and he gently escorted her down a winding cobblestone path to a backless, rough-hewn wooden bench. Jesus sat, raised Mule onto his lap, and nestled her head against his shoulder.

And Jesus spoke: "I'm filled with pride because you turned to me and believed in me, and I helped you to get rid of Luther. And you all carried out my orders so very well. I know you thought it was all over after the baptism, but you have to remember that Satan tried to tempt me three times after mine. Satan is such a jealous fool. He makes me very angry, but he never learns.

"I'm so very happy because now you've proven your love to me. Because of all my love for my children and my Father, I accepted much pain without question. You've shown me how much you love me by bearing all you have and believing I would save you. So you may not be able to say you love me, but your actions prove you do.

"I'm so pleased with all of you, and you will all get to come to the Garden someday. What a crew."

Mule said, "My head hurts."

Jesus said, "I can bet—such a headache! But you'll get better.

"I know Albert is quite a talker, but at least he makes you think. Albert will still come to you, just as I will if you ask me.

"I know you love me, but I want you to love yourself and move the rock. It takes time and tears, but I've cried too."

Mule said, "Please let me stay."

Jesus said, "No, you have to go back and tell the rest of the crew what I said. The angels will be with all of you always, just as I will. Now go and tell them I love them very much."

Part V

Moving the Rock

(July 25, 1984 – August 20, 1984)

There's nothing I enjoy more than walking with my children. I take good care of my children.

– Jesus

Chapter 21

The Commission

July 25, 1984

Albert delivered instructions for the celebration of Satan's defeat: "When ye invite someone into your home to share together in fellowship, it is an expression of love, care, and much joy. Be it of great pleasure that ye shall join together for the breaking of bread and sharing of blessed food; for once again, Communion is desired for ye. It is of Divine right to nourish the body as has the soul been. The Last Supper held importance of great magnitude for Jesus: bestow he upon ye these blessings."

After the celebration, Albert said, "Be there much rejoicing among the angels to see ye gathered together in the arms of the Lord for fellowship and celebration. He showers down much pride and love upon ye, for to obey a Divine request is to show love and respect."

Albert spoke to Farmer: "A prophet is appointed his knowledge from the Lord. If a prophet speaketh of what he knows, and be it of good faith, the Lord's heart abounds with much joy; for to tell of ye knowledge is to further the truth. If but one sheep is gathered, it is not in vain. What difference does it make if the tablet be of stone or paper when the words come from the same place? To share in truth is a most noble thing; for ye shall stand strong, and no amount of wind shall destroy ye.

"When speaking of the Lord, 'tis best to be of clear voice and simple example so all may grow in his Word. Be it not a wise thing to water but one flower to please ye own eye, when they be several in the garden. Would it not be more pleasing to the eye for the hillside to be of intense color for all to see?"

I said, "Albert, it would take me many years to write about this experience."

Albert said: "When the composer knows of a good melody, write it down he must: for to hide the joy of the sound from others is to rob them of their hearing. What good is it to keep a special melody from others, for much happiness it may bring them if they wish to try to play. A tune doesn't have to be famous to be loved, but it must be heard for the musician to choose. The best of symphonies were not composed in a day, thus some consumed in time six years or more. But behold the works of the masters: for they shall survive long after man has died."

Albert then said, "Tell me, who is the daughter of Solomon?"

I said, "The Bible reveals that Taphath is the daughter of Solomon."

Albert said: "The lesson be that she fought for a cause that seemed most time consuming, yet there was importance of its completion. 'Twas a mighty chore, for she worked upon building a garden in the desert; for though it seemed impossible, as mentioned, it was worthwhile. Though the name be published, the deed be not written clearly. Thus I tell ye 'twas a project most worthy of completion; just as the words ye shall put forth be worthy of completion, though it may go unrecognized to some realms within the world. Yet those who know shall be enriched.

THE COMMISSION   123

"If Solomon had not had his daughter, the line of descendants would have been changed; thus in essence, things are meant to be as they are for the outcome is known."

I said, "Will anyone believe the astounding revelations of the book? Most humans have trouble with just the basics."

Albert said, "Be assured there will be much controversy and conflict; for as always, there be those of immediate belief and those demanding proof of unnecessity, just as in the days of the Master. In every jungle, one must be aware of the bamboo shoots, which are the people eager not to listen to the truth, for they shall attack it much like that of a wild beast. Yet in every jungle there be an occasional hibiscus which shall welcome the sweet new of the air. The exceptions in life are far sweeter in one than many evil banded together, for this be a sage of ages."

I said, "Like with Taphath, it seems like a mighty chore."

Albert said: " 'Tis best for the Farmer to take hoe in hand and labor in the field of his desire: for to cultivate a garden with that of vigilance is to be assured a harvest which shall flourish till the wane of countable time and thus be enjoyed by many. Times of hardship yield endurance, yet the outcome shall be of great worth. One may take note of the wildflowers: for though they grow in rugged soils, their beauty shows the victory over the odds of the land.

"When a man desires to hear the word of the Lord, he must clear every hurdle so as to let his way be clear. The ability for ye to hear and understand is of utmost importance, for the bliss of eternity shall be assured for many; thus ye must measure the importance of worldly things wisely. Far richer be the man of poverty: for he may spend his time in meditation on words of wisdom, while the wealthy may squander it sailing the seven seas.

" 'Tis better to be a fisherman of souls: For the catch weighs more and the meat be of a divine sweetness unlike any other known to the palate of man. Thus also, the nourishing lasts eternally, multiplying in goodness. Heavy labor, done of faith, brings about the best of harvests with souls being the fruit: for when the fisherman casts his nets into the sea, and his catch is of plenty, it takes two men to pull the net in—as when something is heavy for one, another must come to his aid—thus both shall share in the catch.

"And as it is with a fisherman who enjoys the water, so it is with ye: For to speculate on the catch be just as much fun. A fisherman enjoys well his sport."

I asked, "Will I receive the gift of the word of knowledge instead of having to use Mule as an intermediary?"

Albert said: "A house with all its adornments made neath the hand of the Eminent Carpenter would stand unto itself containing all perfections in trim so as even the passerby would not look in awe. For 'tis much like a shiny bowl of silver encased behind the glass: too precious to touch, thus appearing most unbelievable."

I said, "So it wouldn't be a good idea, would it?"

Albert said: "To see great perfection is to question the essence of reality: For though the Master roamed the earth, many did not believe until the time in which he arose. Thus for the human man that would contain all gifts, there would be much ridicule and nonbelief, for the heathen world scoffs at the Godlike model. Thus, though some may be given gifts, 'tis for the ways in which they use them best; and one may not have all, for he would appear most inhuman."

I said, "How am I to proceed?"

Albert said: "As it is with moss on a tree in that of a forest, the deeper into the forest ye may travel, the thicker be the moss. This be in that of understanding: for the more you absorb, the greater and richer ye may impart upon others. Understanding evolves into that of knowledge, for one who knows truly understands.

"The mountain from a distance is breathtaking, yet along the way there is curious vegetation. When unsure, do not pick it, but know well that it is there and what its scents are. Go about the mountain terrain much like that of the rugged tiger: for though he be a tiger, he sees the beauty and enjoys the fresh air, though he has paws of iron. 'Tis also much like that of being with a skin of thickness: for though the arrows be annoying, they penetrate not to thus crumble the character.

"Remember: A tree growing within its elements is not endangered, much like that of an animal rare in species. For to move it out of the boundaries of familiarity is to endanger it; yet to let it run about its territory is of vague safety. Ye be the rarest of species for the knowledge of which ye know. For a rare bird to roost in another's territory is of great plight: for to not be familiar is most antagonizing."

Chapter 22

Rock-Moving Visions

July 31, 1984

Albert spoke to Mule: "A coal miner works hard, but he gets paid well for his work and soon shall ye. For there is much pain to the coal miner's muscles, but the harder the pick falls, the bigger the chunk that is plucked away. The coal is heavy, but it serves a purpose.

"A coal miner goes into the dark of willingness and comes out with much accomplishment. His sweat is but the cloak of his efforts. He greets the light with joy, only to go down into the dark again, for he knows his purpose. Take note he never goes down alone: for if he did and something happened, he wouldn't have a hand to lead him out. Be he grateful that he can submerge into the mine with a human buddy and a Divine One. Though he can protect his head with a helmet, his heart is shielded with the Holy Spirit.

"When a coal miner has much work to do, he comes up for air for a while. The heart of a miner is special because not everyone would go into the mine, for many would fear never to return."

As usual, Mule resisted her rock-moving instructions.

Albert said: "When a newborn babe is held, it has not the knowledge of being dropped, and thus it is relaxed and content. Sometimes be it necessary to have strength to hold: it matters not whether 'tis of physical, mental, or emotional; for at times, all may be needed depending upon the chore, but to receive is blessed. When sheltered in strong arms, there be no need for fear; thus, to struggle is but energy wasted, hindering unharnessing of true meanings. To embrace on the outside with grace of arms is to but reach into the soul of the inside and send forth much care of tender."

Mule said, "It still hurts to hold close to him, Albert."

Albert spoke firmly: "When a mule moves down his ears, he's not listening. To bray is a much annoying sound. If ye must be a mule, at least accept a rider, for at least he can kick you. 'Twould be best not to use spurs, but in desperate times, it may be necessary: for the mule be loaded with fruit in his baskets, and 'tis necessary to get it to the ship on time."

Mule said, "But I'm so tired, and this is all so strange. I'm different than everybody else, and I don't like it."

Albert said, "To be a sheep of black is not to be of disgrace, but distinction."

I said, "Mule is a handful, isn't she, Albert?"

Albert said: "When in the times of the Indians roaming the vast countryside, the papoose left not its mother: for strapped to her, it fed, napped, and grew in spirit. If it were not cared for in such a way, death in the wilderness would have been evident. To develop a spirit and complete chores, this was a most wise method. A wise Indian praised the Lord in many ways, knowing always of the blessings of sun, moon, and mother earth."

I said, "Are you suggesting that I should watch Mule even more closely than I already am?"

Albert said: "When a shepherd keeps watch of his flock, he does so by day and night. At the moment he notices one has gone astray or be there a source of troubled mind of one, he shall go in search of it. If he were to come across a stray sheep caught by the picks of a fence, he would not stand useless, but respond to its cries by administering aid, thus helping it loose of its bind.

"Many miles be wandered, thus mishaps be of no surprise. But a shepherd so cares for his sheep, he repeats his acts many a time. All shall arrive at the destination safely, though a few straggle along timidly."

"But, Albert," I said, "sometimes Mule will just not cooperate. I know this is often because of the demons' influence, but I am reluctant to be too forceful with her."

Albert said: "If a master lets his dog out and does not watch over it, it may come back with burdocks. A dog may enjoy his freedom, but he will pay for it later, for 'tis painful to have unwanted things removed. But if so knoweth the master, to groom his dog is not to punish, for it is but to return the fur to shininess. For 'twould a mule move faster if he had a burr on his butt? A good dog knows the master's help is needed, for he cannot pour the food himself, nor drink of the water from the spigot.

"When a master takes his dog for a swim, he must approach shallow waters for the dog not to panic; for to throw him in would not be of much assurance if he could not swim. 'Tis best to lead him into shallow waters first and then proceed. Be the master of good instinct, for the dog shall learn this. Yet at times, the master must grab the dog by the scruff of the neck, but 'tis of care and not hate.

"As the master and his dog grow together, it is not only the mind of the dog that grows, for a good master may learn of himself through his dog: for if one cries and the other tastes the salt, there is a merging of the souls known only to the Divine; thus is entwined a bond of special value."

Mule clamped her hands over her ears. "Do you think Albert would make the children stop singing?"

"Oh, no, Mule," I groaned. "You're not hearing Luther's children again are you?"

Mule said, "No." She placed her hands over her eyes and said, "Tell Albert to stop the pictures too."

Albert said, "Be ye, oh, so stubborn."

I asked, "What is happening, Mule? I don't understand."

Mule said: "I see myself in kindergarten, and all the kids are around me, and they are teasing me. It's just like I am there right now. I can see everything just as it was, hear everything just like it was, and I feel just the way I did then. Tell Albert to stop it."

I checked for demons, but Mule was clean. The angels were showing her a vision of her first year in school, down to the finest detail.

Mule narrated: "Now some kids are asking me to play with them, but I don't want to. I'm scared of them, but they won't leave me alone. They are calling me bad names like *'fraidy cat*. Tell Albert to stop showing me these pictures."

I said, "Mule, just watch the pictures and tell me what happens, and we will talk about it later."

Mule continued: "I want to play alone in the corner, but the teacher won't let me. The kids are laughing at me and being real mean."

Mule began to cry softly and moaned, "The rock is getting heavier."

Albert clarified the purpose of the visions: Mule had a rock heart not only because of the traumas caused by evil, but because she had suppressed the pain. Now, with the aid of a Divine microscope, she would be forced to reexperience the pain in a protected environment and cry her tears. This would provide the necessary lubrication to help budge the rock. From now on, in addition to my holding Mule as before, our sessions would include these rock-moving visions.

Mule described the final scene of the rock-moving vision, spanning ages four to six: "And now the mean doctor wants me to give my dog away because he sheds hair, and that's not good for my health. Don't let him give my dog away, mommy. I'll be real good, and I won't get sick. Oh, no, there goes my dog." By now, Mule was sobbing quite heavily.

Katrina said, "It's okay. It's all in the past now."

Albert said, "Despite the well-known characteristics of the mule, ye attain characteristics most similar to that of a turtle: For if not prodded, the turtle would be content to dwell in the sand all the day long. And ye be of a most withdrawn nature, quite like the turtle retracting his head from the view of the waters and sealing out the inmost thoughts within a hardened shell of the fear of predators curious of the makings of ye house. Yet a turtle is a gentle creature which floats gently in the waters of kindness."

I said to Albert, "It is amazing God has recorded our lives in such detail."

Albert said, "If 'tis possible for years to flash by in that of one day, imagine days in relation to the marvel of eternity."

"I do try to imagine, Albert," I sighed. "I do try."

Albert said, "The keeper of the dam is always most busy during the flood season; thus until the storms have passed, he must execute supreme care knowing rewards shall come to pass when a new season evolves. Glorious pastures and rolling green meadows shall await him. He shall roam amidst the wildflowers elated with joy, for it has been foretold from Above."

Albert taught that Holy Spirit grew by the same principles as a farmer's crop: there was always the need for good seed, fertile soil, adequate watering, weed control, etc. Metaphorically, yet also in a very practical sense, Mule and I were workers of the field.

Albert spoke to Mule: "Be ye more like the plow horse, for it is strong and works hard to leave behind it furrows to plant new things. The plow horse obeys the Farmer and asks not for carrots, for the Farmer knows best when feeding time arrives.

"'Tis best the Farmer knows the planting season, for the plow horse would be most happy at pasture. But the Farmer knows when 'tis best to store his barn of hay, for would he make the horse work if there be nothing to eat at sunset?

"After the crops are sown, both shall rest and anticipate the joys of the harvest, for then the value of the work is most truly known. And the Farmer and his horse shall both benefit, for they both work together, and both shall share in the crop.

"When the season comes and 'tis time for the Farmer and his horse to be at the pastures, they will have earned it: for one that had not worked his way there would not find the realms of joy as in that of the learned one. To graze upon the meadowlands and gallop across the valley to the bluffs shall come to be a most restful pleasure when the labors be done.

"And as it has been, to look after one solicitously with the passages of time thus forms a covenant not to be broken: for this be so of the Farmer and his horse."

As the rock-moving visions continued, so too did the waxing of the moon. The panicked demons picked up their pace.

Albert spoke: "The mysteries of the moon hold many a spell. The wicked dance beneath the beams of the mighty moon, for there be a power known only to them in which they take great joy and thus worship accordingly. Follow the moon to its fullness, for the moon has a mystical drawing power.

"As one labors intensely, keeping a watchful eye upon the filling of the moon, he may let his heart fill in equal portions with the knowledge that the gleaming beauty of the full moon shall cast a warm radiance upon a cleared path. Be it known that such a path will house many pebbles; however, let them not ensue into that of growth into a rock. One must work hard to achieve this.

"Fear not, for to follow instructions is to be assured. I say unto you to follow the moon and the Master's commands."

Chapter 23

The Demon of Hate

August 6, 1984

Mule's voice snarled at me over the phone: "I'm not coming over to your office today. I'm sick of all this angel and God business, and I am sick of you."

I yawned and continued to thumb through the sports scores in the newspaper. "Is that so?"

"Yes, that's so," Mule's voice spat back.

I said, "You have to come over to the office, even if you don't want to."

Mule's voice growled, "No, I don't. I think the authorities need to be made aware of your unethical methods of treatment. They don't believe in demons."

I laughed and said, "That's because there are so many of your kind amongst them."

"What do you mean, 'my kind'?" Mule's voice challenged. The dullard demon had not yet realized that I was onto its transparent masquerade.

I said, "This has been fun. I've enjoyed our little chat. But now it's time to come over."

The dullard demon paused to consider whether its cover was blown. Still masquerading behind Mule's voice and personality, the demon said, "You won't see me there no matter how long you wait."

I said, "Yes, I will see you, because in the name of Jesus, I command you to bring her here safely. I further command that any demonic opposition to this command be punished in the same manner as Luther." After a long silence, the phone disconnected. I knew from much experience that Mule was on her way and would arrive safely.

My ability to discern evil spirits was a gift from God. But like most God-given gifts, it began as a seed and had to be nourished through much practice. I had always had the seed. Even in my early days with Mule, Luther had not hidden his presence from me; yet how was I to know that the knot in the pit of my stomach was the clash of the Holy Spirit within me against the evil spirit who possessed her? Until I understood this association, my gift would lie dormant.

However, now, under Divine guidance and training, I had developed into a bloodhound of discernment. Whenever I caught the slightest whiff of evil in Mule, I simply checked for demons. There was no need to speculate over whether or not she was possessed or influenced.

I had learned the golden rule of discernment: when in doubt, check it out. If demons were present, they would have to obey (eventually) the commands given them in the name of Jesus; if demons were not present, no harm was done. If Mule resisted the test, she was possessed or influenced; for in her true spirit, she never resisted.

Most demons had made an adjustment because of my developing skills and confidence. In contrast to their previous bravado, they usually went to extraordinary lengths to blend unnoticed into Mule's personality. Without detection, there would be no confrontation; and without confrontation, they could roost as long as they wanted.

The demon who now possessed Mule was surely an aggressive one, for it had made no attempt to hide behind less hostile words. The only reason it continued the pretense of speaking through Mule's voice was because the demonic instinct for deception was so deeply ingrained. Demons would always keep up pretense (transparent though it might be) until forced to do otherwise. There was much to be gained from pondering this principle.

I opened my office door, and Mule brusquely swept past me. She threw herself onto the cushioned armchair, and her bulging eyes fixed me with a malevolent stare.

Through clenched teeth, Mule's masquerading demon spat, "Well, I'm here. Now what?"

I pulled my chair directly in front of Mule's and pinioned her wrists to the arms of her chair. "Demon, in the name of Jesus, I command you to quit hiding behind her personality and confront me."

Mule's voice replied, "Oh, shut up. There's no one here."

I said, "The command has been given. For every second you delay, I ask Jesus to kill a suitable number of demons in response to your disobedience to the command."

Mule's eyelids immediately closed. Her body gradually puffed up like an expanding balloon. She arched her back and hovered over me like a predatory cat about to pounce.

I knew I was in for a fight. Demons of this ilk did not voluntarily vacate captured territory; they had to be evicted.

I again commanded, "Demon, come forth. In the name of Jesus, I give the command."

Suddenly, the demon lashed out at me with such strength it toppled me backward over my chair onto the floor. It landed on top of me, scrambled to its feet, and made a dash for the door. From my prone position, I grabbed its ankle and held firm, causing it to reel and fall on me in a heap. We wrestled for position, and I somehow managed to come out on top. It took all my weight and strength to keep the powerful possessing spirit pinned.

The demon began to thrash Mule's head against the floor with concussive effect. "Hate, hate, hate," the demon spoke with each blow.

For the moment, Mule did not feel the head blows, for the demon had evicted the essence of her soul to a holding space in Hell—and only the current tenant need pay rent. Yet when she returned, she would most definitely feel the effects, so I cushioned her head as best I could.

However, the demon *did* feel the blows as it was inflicting them. The demon was now the official tenant of Mule's body, under legal obligation to landlord Jesus, because I had commanded it to quit hiding and come forth, thus unraveling the intertwined spirits. If the demon had not been so commanded, it could have beaten Mule's head all day long and not felt a thing. I had been taught to always separate (by command) the demonic spirit(s) from the captive spirit, and in the case of multiple demons, to also separate them one from another—then, to defeat them in detail. Yet this demon was willing to exchange some temporary pain to itself (as long as it was in Mule's body), for a longer-lasting pain or injury to Mule after it departed.

All demons knew well the bind this created: If I were too aggressive in restraint in response to their provocations, I might inflict some damage that Mule would feel when she returned; if I were too passive, they would inflict the damage themselves. It was just one of the endless double binds that were a routine part of dealing with evil.

So sometimes, despite my best efforts to use effective techniques with the demons, Mule and I inflicted some damage upon each other in our rough and tumble. Whenever this happened, Jesus assisted us in healing. I had enough experience with the athletic injuries of my youth to know the rapid recovery went far beyond the normal healing process.

After I dispatched the feisty demon, the essence of Mule's soul returned to her physical body.

When I turned to place a displaced book upon my desk, Mule giggled, despite the ordeal she had just been through. "What are you laughing at, Mule?" I asked.

Mule said, "Your pants are ripped out in the bottom."

Returning the joke, I said, "You are no prize yourself." Her skirt, originally buttoned down the front, now buttoned down the back.

Albert said, "Be wary of creatures of the dark."

I asked, "What demon was that?"

Albert replied, "The Demon of Hate." (*Generic demons have no gender. Although this was one specific Demon of Hate, there are millions of demons of hate.*)

Mule asked, "Albert, why do the angels let these demons continue to possess me? I don't understand."

Albert replied, "We are glad to help, yet ye must fight for what ye believe in."

Mule asked, "How much longer will this continue?"

Albert said, "Be there much pride when the cherry blossoms fall."

Mule looked at me and asked, "Don't the cherry blossoms fall in the spring?"

I wearily nodded my head yes. After two months of intense struggle with evil, we had at least seven more months to go.

Albert empathized, "Bone-weary soldiers shall give support unto each other while marching on for a cause. Giving of life unto one another be a vital blessing bestowed upon ye by the Divine."

Albert instructed: "Be it known that creatures of darkness find pleasure in habitating neath shades of rocks. Be they scared, for to lose shade is to allow light to enter; thus as a rock grasps forward, its residents of shade may labor to enter in and cover up by closing its hole. Fear not, for the light shall blind them until they flee in agony. Remember: Weary soldiers march on for a cause. To be united is not to be defeated.

"Be it also known that creatures who dwell in the deepest part of the forest enjoy scampering about in the darkness of shadows. Also, many a contented snake slumbers neath the cool dampness of rocks. Thus when territories be disturbed to break ground for pathways leading to a temple, the inhabitants scurry frantically for a deeper section of the forest.

"The brightest of light shall penetrate the darkest of the wooded lands. Alas, 'twould be of greater ease when the trail be but roughly blazed. Many a creature may stray across the path, but heed to warnings and flee: this be so until the path leads to the Land of the Fadeless Day.

"So as the star of long ago led the wise men, allow the moon to guide ye in the rough blazing of a path."

Chapter 24

The Demon of Lust

August 8, 1984

The possession was instantaneous: One moment Mule had been calm and peaceful, but now she giggled like an immature schoolgirl. Her eyes were opened wider than I had ever seen them, and her eyelashes fluttered furiously. She primped her hair and turned towards me in a seductive posture. Although Mule's body was before me, her spirit was not.

I quickly asserted authority: "Demon, I command you to acknowledge that Jesus is Lord."

The demon batted its eyelashes and said, "Why everyone knows that. What's the point in saying the obvious?"

"Admit that I am united with Jesus," I commanded.

The coquettish demon said, "Well, of course, sweetie. You like to beat the obvious to death, don't you?"

"What's your name, demon?"

The demon began to stroke my knee. It purred, "Oh, you know me, you big hunk of man. My name is Lust. Want to play? I know lots of games, and you have such a cute butt."

Though Lust offered little physical threat, I pinned it to the ground as a precaution. "Owww, you are hurting me," it

139

protested. "We all know you like to play rough. Go get some rope and tie me up, and we can play as rough as you like."

The Demon of Lust was so exaggerated in its seductiveness that I was sickened, even more so than with the more outwardly aggressive demons. For the next half hour, it continued to tempt me into having sex, while I did my best to dispatch it with prayer.

When the phone rang, Lust shouted out, "Go ahead and answer the phone! Maybe Jesus is on the phone, and I can tempt him!"

"Why don't you go tempt Luther instead?" I said. "He's in the pit where you belong."

Lust said, "I didn't know Luther was in the pit, but we used to play together a lot. We even played with her. You didn't know about that, did you? But I can show you. Come on, everyone does it."

"Jesus didn't," I replied.

Lust laughed uproariously. "Well, the reason that Jesus didn't do it was that I never personally tempted him. But you are a different story. Go ahead and get some rope. All hell knows you like to play rough."

I had to take a break from this vile spirit. I placed my hand tightly over its mouth and read aloud from the Bible.

Lust's muffled voice screamed, "I don't know why you try to fight me. I know you want to do it. I'm telling you that you want to do it."

I said, "Be gone, demon, in the name of Jesus."

Lust's vanity was wounded. "You read too many books, honey. Come on and let's have some fun."

As I continued to read the Bible, Lust commented, "Even Jesus wanted to do it, because if he wandered about in the desert for forty days, he must have wanted to do it. Do you know what I mean?"

I said, "Jesus died for our sins."

Lust interjected, "Oh, yeah, I must admit that is very true. I actually saw him on the cross. That was some day. Did you know that he didn't even have a shirt on, and oooh-boy, what a chest."

The Demon of Lust was quite a piece of filth. "Jesus was without sin," I sternly returned, "and you are unworthy to speak his name."

"He wasn't pure," Lust bluffed. "No one is pure. Who are you trying to kid? And she is a little tramp."

I said, "Whatever she is, she shall spend eternity in Heaven. And let me be clear here: you won't."

"Come on," Lust shrilled. "You really don't care about her. You're only worried she will refuse she knows you before the rooster crows twice, and then you won't get your book written."

As the battle finally drew to a close, Lust departed with a warning, "I'll get you, sweetie. No one can resist me forever."

Mule returned, and Albert said, "Ye, Farmer, be much like that of a cat in the alley, pouncing upon those lingering neath the shadow of the disposal cans: for these cats be of great value in the extermination of needless mice."

I said, "Albert, there has been quite the congregation of evil spirits here lately."

And Albert spoke of the impending Evil Party: "Though creatures may masquerade about, the party may not last forever. Like that of any gathering of disguise, 'tis difficult for the host to identify the attendants; but fear not, for sober be the guest who can, and he shall unveil the impersonators. To identify is to become keenly aware, thus most knowledge comes with study and practice. When a party is of much fun, most guests hate to leave, but the hours dwindle down until the dawn.

"With the season of the parties, 'tis most difficult to make a choice of which ones to attend. Some go to all, but eventually tire. The most wild of parties take place in the darkest of night, for impersonators thrive in disguise with the cloak of midnight. Be there always one who takes precedence, thus becoming the life of the party.

"They shall have an end on the night when the fullness of the moon sheds its light upon them in unison with the Holy Light. Be there a most intense spotlight which shall send them blindly fleeing."

Chapter 25

The Evil Party

August 11, 1984 (day and night of the full moon)

Upon the dawn, Albert spoke of the evening's party arrangements: "We shall not take up sword against them, but the weapon of laughter. Evil impostors at any party cannot withstand that of holy laughter. 'Tis more enjoyable to be of laughter than to fight of sword, yet accomplish the same purpose. Michael (the angel) says, at times, this be a weapon more powerful than a sword, especially when dealing with fools of vanity.

"Ye shall find this to be a party of working, but seek enjoyment in knowing that it be a party of farewell, for this your toils are worth. Be it known that for the masquerading guests, 'tis much like a surprise party: for when the light shines upon them all, it proves all their hopes be but false. Some guests arrive early, and then there are those who arrive late, but they are all gone when the dawn comes.

"Most parties have no set agenda, for 'tis unpredictable to schedule events when one knows not what the guests may like for fun. However, be it known that those wishing to play games on holy turf may never achieve triumph, for they be in great defeat before the games even commence.

"Be it important to sharpen the mind with that of the Holy Spirit: for to mingle with the guests takes much care of inspection. Yet when watching and confronting the guests, forget not your host.

"Children of God may have reunions in the Holy Family. Members of the Holy Family bring not cakes and pies, for they follow the Rites, be they of so much important value: for to follow the Rites is to share in Christ as earthly children share in their father; yet to follow the Rites be most glorious and of eternal value.

"A family reunion of this kind be more important than a party. But when it is ended, ye may go to a party not in fear, for God's children shall leave the party hand in hand in victory. Thus 'tis best to attend the reunion before going to a party."

Mule begged Albert, "Please don't leave me today."

Albert said, "I maketh plans ye need not concern yourself with. But I shall guide you as I am told, for I love you very much."

Throughout the remainder of the day, Mule viewed rock-moving visions of her high school and young adult years. This panicked the demons, for the more that Mule understood and accepted the truth of her life, the less spiritual darkness there was to hide them. Therefore, during the time of lull between visions, a multitude of evil spirits tried to hinder her progress. It was exhausting to Mule and me to focus on the visions *and* fight off demons.

As night arrived, the demon attacks and our fatigue made it impossible to attend to the visions. The demons eventually overran Mule's soul and possessed her body. I was left to confront what came.

The demon spoke, "Oh boy, I love to set fires. Love it. Let's set a fire and burn bodies."

I asked, "What's your name, demon?"

"Arson," it replied. "Do you know the Demon of Hate? It is here too. Wherever there is Arson, there is Hate. I'm going to go find Hate."

"Lies, lies, we all lie," the Demon of Lies spoke. "Lying is so much fun."

I said, "Be gone, all you wicked demons, in the name of Jesus."

They said, "We don't like Jesus."

Suddenly, the Demon of Lies cocked its head to the side. "Oh, they are laughing at me; the angels are laughing at me. I'm leaving."

When the Demon of Lies departed, another demon took its place. "I love to cause nagging pains," the demon squealed. "Headache here, stomach ache there, pain all over."

Another demon came to the fore and joined in, "Hot, hot, hot; it's so hot in Hell."

And so it went with the excitable party guests: in and out, back and forth, one after the other. More demons than I care to remember, but all their father's children.

During a brief respite, Albert spoke: "Most have gone home because they only came in curiosity. Ones of importance shall be fleeing soon. They've been trying to seek refuge among the shadows of the moonlight. It's been out in fullness so long, the intensity has grown immense. There be very few shadows to hide among.

"They cast a shadow neath the rock, for 'tis at the edge of the path. It will take a little longer to move, but it has been turned in smoothness. 'Tis smooth from wear. Creatures may clingeth not upon a smooth surface that has been lathed by the hand of God.

"Moonlight may shine through windows. 'Tis much like that of Holy Light, for it can shine if there is but the tiniest of openings. If ye think of the beauty of a moonlit room, ye can only but imagine the gloriousness of the Holy Light within a soul."

Mule said, "This is all kind of scary, Albert."

Albert said, "Fear not, for the heavenly armies are in multitudes bearing the weapon of laughter. Ye shall only see them leaving, for we are standing ready. Several have fled that ye have not known about, for 'tis easy to mock an immature fool and send them fleeing."

I asked, "How many demons are left, Albert?"

Albert said, "Hate, Violence, and Lust."

In its best attempt at a seductive voice, the Demon of Lust said, "Hello again, honey."

"Not you again," I groaned in disgust.

Lust said, "Don't be like that; I'm the life of the party. Ready for some good sex now?"

I said, "Go away, you wicked spirit."

"Oh, no," it protested, "you have it all wrong. I'm not a wicked spirit; I'm a fun spirit."

I said, "Go away anyway."

Lust said, "Did you know that I know all about Albert? I don't know why he doesn't like me. He's giving me a dirty look right now."

I said, "It's because you are so disgusting, even for a demon."

Lust scolded: "Jesus has made you such a bore, lover boy. Everyone falls to temptation. Do you really believe in the Virgin Birth? That's one for the fairy tale books. Oh, well, I guess I will leave for now, but you know I can always come back."

Lust departed, and the Demon of Hate immediately took its place. It snarled, "Hate is powerful, powerful, powerful." It reached up and tried to grasp Mule's cross necklace which hung around her neck.

"No, you don't," I said as I stopped Hate's hand short of its goal.

Hate said, "I hate you, wicked man. I would really like to kill you. My friend, Violence, would help me do it too. Violence is around here somewhere."

Abruptly, the expression on Hate's face changed to shame. "The angels are laughing at me—at *me*. Oh, I have to go," Hate said as it made its exit.

The Demon of Violence immediately came forth and tomahawked me on the head with bruising force. "Kill the wicked man!" Violence shouted.

"In the name of Jesus, I bind your power," I huffed through sweaty lips. "Be gone in the name of Jesus."

Violence screamed, "Oh…" and its voice trailed off.

The Demon of Lust spoke, "It's so dark in here. But as you know, I really like to work in the dark."

I said, "Be gone in the name of Jesus, you vile demon."

Lust lectured, "It's always Jesus, Jesus, Jesus, with you. What's your problem? Let's have sex. I admit Jesus was sinless, but no one else is. But he's not around now."

Suddenly, Jesus reached down from Heaven, grasped the rock, and cast it aside like a ball. This illuminated Mule's path with Holy Light, leaving no more shadows to hide the demons.

Lust said, "Oh, no, there's a light that's on now. I can see the angels. There's Albert over there. Say, these angel guys are good looking. Do you angels want to have sex with me?"

Katrina and Lucinda appeared and grabbed onto Lust's limbs. "Let me go, you stinking angels," Lust howled. "I have a right to be here because she was filled with darkness. Don't laugh at me; don't laugh at me. Katrina and Lucinda, you have no right to laugh at me."

Finally, silence. It was 5:20 a.m., August 12, 1984.

Katrina and Lucinda escorted the essence of Mule's soul to the entrance of Heaven's Garden where Jesus awaited.

And Jesus spoke: "I know it's been hard, but you've both done so very well. I've cast the rock aside like I promised. There are a few large pieces you still have to move, and then it's just a matter of sorting out the pebbles. Be patient, because from the size of the rock, there are a lot of pebbles to sort through. Remember to never build another rock, because it gives Satan and his foolish children places to hide.

"The worst sins to fall to are hate, violence, and lust. I don't like them, but if my children are sincerely sorry, I'll always forgive them.

"It will take a while to make the path smooth, but now that you have it started, I can walk the rest of the way with you. There's nothing I enjoy more than walking with my children. I take good care of my children. Just remember to ask for me, and I'll always come."

Mule pleaded with Jesus, "Please let me stay this time."

Jesus said, "You'll be able to come, but not now. I promise you'll come here. You don't belong to the Dark Side. I'm so very proud to see how hard you've worked because you believe. That demonstrates a lot of love."

With playful humor, Jesus said, "I know you are both very tired, and now maybe you won't have to rough each other up so much. So go in peace."

Upon Mule's return, Albert said: "It matters not where on earth ye live, or as to how far away ye are, for as long as ye ask, Jesus will always come."

Chapter 26

The Imps

August 12, 1984

Albert instructed Mule on the next phase of her deliverance: "How wonderful be the triumph ye have achieved in that of setting in motion the immense rock; now that they be but chunks left, 'tis still of necessity to move them also. As it is after all parties, the chore of making tidy is so tedious; thus listen to the voice of reason.

"Be not startled if an evil imp darts across the path, for it be in that of a flash, as weak eyes adapt not to intense light. Be it known that this may happen; hence do not be weak of prayer.

"Look to the one who helps you, as for the time at hand 'tis not expected for ye to stand alone; remember that of a newborn colt. For when the rocks be unbroken, tiny creatures may dwell in the smallest of shades."

I consulted the dictionary and saw that an imp was defined as a small demon. I asked Albert, "Are imps easier to dispatch because of their small size?"

Albert said, "Their powers be just as those with characteristics of fullness, yet they be more pesky in nature than that of a full-created spirit. Imps be creations of afterthought."

I said, "Are you saying that Satan creates imps by a process known as afterthought?"

Albert said, "Yes, for Satan has a mimicking skill which be that of blowing the breath of life into them."

I asked, "What is the primary function of imps?"

Albert said, "A thought in the mind doubting oneself, and turning against one his own thoughts, is but the hinting voices of the imps. 'Tis best to never underestimate the power of the imps: for though they be small, they cast a mighty shadow. Paul knew well of these thorns."

I asked, "Were imps the thorns that Paul spoke of in the Bible?"

Albert said, "Yes, for perhaps there be many attacks on the mind, even on the purest and most intentional of souls."

The imps devised a deviously effective strategy to block Mule's progress: They continuously whispered self-destructive thoughts in her mind that drained her energy and resistance. She would succumb by falling into a deep sleep, a sleep so deep that she could not be awakened by normal means. In this state, she could neither pray, nor attend to the rock-moving visions.

Countering the imps' strategy presented me with a tactical challenge: First, they were much more difficult to discern than fully developed demons. Their initial influences on Mule were sometimes so subtle that I would not suspect that anything was amiss until they had completely overcome her faculties. Second, once entrenched, the imps were difficult to provoke into confrontations without hours of prayer. My growing fatigue made this type of effort nearly impossible, at least on a consistent basis.

On one occasion, however, I was able to confront an imp directly. I said, "Mule, I want you to read the Bible for me."

As Mule began to read, a great weariness engulfed her. "I can't do this anymore," she said.

I insisted, "Come on, Mule; you know you must."

Mule struggled to follow my instructions, but the imps overwhelmed her faculties, and she fell stone asleep in the middle of a sentence.

I said, "In the name of Jesus, I command you to come out, imp."

A very high-pitched, almost comical, voice spoke, "Leave me alone. I just want to be left alone."

I said, "You are not allowed to bother her. Be gone in the name of Jesus."

Suddenly, the demon began to struggle with me using strength much greater than the name of imp would imply. The imp squealed: "I didn't mean to. It was a mistake for you to catch me. It is safe in here. Just let me go, and I won't bother her anymore."

After the demon was dispatched, Albert said, "Those chained in prisons of darkness be best suited to remain there, for the light will inflict unbearable torment upon them. Be they much like a bat in a cave."

I said, "Albert, I thought imps were supposed to be little demons, but that one was strong."

Albert said, "Intensity may not necessarily be measured in that of volume, for great power contained in a tiny space may be more effective than strength abiding in a space of much immenseness."

August 17, 1984

Albert delivered the word of the Lord to Mule: "Consider this not that of a recommendation, but an order: that the rock fragments be dislodged from the path before the moon fades of fullness for a few nights, for time spent in slumber and laziness is but time for evil imps to call to arms all of their forces. Foolish cowards multiply and attack in the dark; thus if enough were to gather and push the fragments together, they will overtake the sleeping sentry. Since they be of such smallness, to recognize them be a most difficult chore.

"Angels may help in that of protection, but not in that of pushing, for they have not been summoned to. Be of no misunderstanding, for ye are not being punished, but helped in a way you may not understand, for that time has not arrived yet.

"The Lord has bestowed his authority to the one who helps you, as he may act however harshly he must in order to accomplish the chore at hand. This be of loving concern and not anger: for sometimes to clear a field, the Farmer must pull a few stumps and burn a few weeds. Yet the knowledgeable Farmer needs not his neighbor to help, for his abilities are greatly strengthened by the Lord.

"Though it seems that rock fragments be of heavy labor to move, be it known that 'tis only but for the edges of sharpness which protrude in the way. Move them you must, for many an evil creature would rather nap in a little shade than that of blaring light. A laborer must not be allowed to fall a'slumber, for it hinders progress.

"Ye be just at the edge of the last row to furrow; thus when the end be in sight and the bones be weary, go forth with knowledge of victory at hand. For it is so that the Farmer is in need of rest, just as his horse. Hence at times, he must be of a stern nature and not allow the horse to halt; for the time to start anew would be at hand, and the crops would be late with little chance to be as bountiful as when planted early.

"It has been said unto ye that the fragments must be moved as to not allow further hibernation of Satan's weary imps. Ye are not to slumber till this chore be accomplished, and then ye shall reap the benefits of rest and that of sorting the pebbles.

These words are of love, though at times you may feel punished. This is not so, for the Lord loves ye and empowers the helper to be as stern as necessary.

"Set ye hopes high, for the rocks have but a few tiny turns left to go until the waters calm for good times. The command has been passed down that 'tis most best to try in these night hours, for the taunting imps would keep on if a span of time were to continue. Victory is assured, and sailing on smooth waters is promised from Above.

"Be aware also that the waters may not always be calm; yet in the future when the waves crest, ease of asking for assistance will help overcome the powers of darkness. Just as a young sapling stands in the elements by itself, help will come to aid with support of stakes when need indicates so.

"After sending fragments along over the edge of a cliff, night visions of the evil impostors may visit. However, if the host is not alone and help be at hand in the physical state, it will ease nightmares; for dark beings resent leaving any space, no matter how small and compact it was. Assurance is given this may only be but for two or so nights until the foolish beings tire of fighting a losing battle and come to realize that Christ is the Almighty One who shall end their games.

"A widow crying in the night shall not be so lonely if aid be at hand. The Lord Jesus is everywhere, but at times the touch of a human hand be of value; and 'tis very important that he requesteth some of his children to be in the presence to aid him in the fulfillment of his desires. To serve the Lord is the most vital of all activities one may fulfill in his lifetime.

"Rest is acknowledged before the time of sorting pebbles comes to be. Time and patience shall be most important, and be it known that several seasons shall pass by before a hearty and healthy garden comes to bloom; but, oh, what splendor to behold when it does, for the host shall, indeed, be a new being fully born into the family of the Lord."

154   MOVING THE ROCK

It was a comedy; it was a tragedy; it was now 7:00 a.m., August 18, 1984. For the past fourteen hours, the angels had shown Mule rock-moving visions, while the imps had urgently tried to make her sleep.

Although Jesus had empowered me to do whatever was necessary to keep Mule awake so she could attend to the visions, I hoped I had not taken him too literally. At times, I had lifted Mule off the ground and shaken her like a rag doll to arouse her. If that didn't work, I doused her head under water. When that became ineffective, I had stepped on her toes. When all other methods failed and Mule was on the verge of falling asleep, I had her inhale noxious substances until she became ill. The angels and Mule made no comments whatsoever on my methods, for they knew my instructions and the importance of keeping Mule awake.

Now, the pummeled Mule finished narrating the final rock-moving vision: "And all of the sickness I had in Texas was because of Luther's influence; and the demons who were at the Evil Party visited me at other times of my life; and now I see you sitting on top of me at the Evil Party, and you are fighting with the demons; and now, the imps are trying to make me sleep."

I said, "Go on, Mule."

Mule said, "Albert said the rock-moving visions are over."

Albert said: "The road has been long, for it was started many years ago. When a road reaches a certain path, it must make a choice, and it has been proven the path to the Lord is the correct path. Those following that path have much victory.

"The rock fragments have been condensed to pebbles just as the Lord promised. Ye need not worry of any more creatures of darkness or imps who inhabit small crevices, for now they be just pebbles.

"The time is at hand when the Lord wishes to speak of the end."

The essence of Mule's soul was transported to Heaven's Garden of Knowledge and Contemplation, where she again met with Jesus.

And Jesus spoke: "I know it's been tough, but many roads worth traveling must be traveled for a worthwhile cause. Now you are to be assured that it's only pebbles that need to be sorted. Don't be discouraged, because that is going to take a long time.

"Tell Farmer I know he's very tired, but I have given him strength he knows not of; for to achieve this task was of much importance so that things may settle down to pebble sorting, which is less trying on him. Also, tell Farmer that I will walk the path with him many times—and not to be discouraged—for he shall see me when the time is right. Indeed, he will see the green pastures.

"As for you, I'm a little concerned because we've pushed you a little faster than needed, but to get the task done, 'twas necessary. I love you very much, as I have said before, and that will never change. Now rest in peace and be aware of the night visions, for these visions you will have in sleep. Time will help make them go away."

Chapter 27

Remember Elizabeth

August 19, 1984

Albert spoke to Mule: "Use much care with that of your head, for you knoweth by now that disturbances of the inner ear create unsteadiness. I forewarn ye of this in hopes ye shall take warning to avoid injury, for at times ye be of a great stubbornness and fall anyway. Mighty shakes of the already injured were done in love and not of harm, but it has been ordered that ye take things in ease for a day or so, then recovery shall swiften.

"Steadiness of feet be not of such importance as that of stillness of head, for to put in motion at times of weakness only might hinder recovery. Ye have not been punished, only given blessed help; for if ye were to have fallen a'slumber in the night of past, all work would have had heavy beginnings again. Holy strength was bestowed upon ye both, and with loving care, Jesus shall renew ye both.

"Jesus knows about ye head. He has the power to heal, but 'tis a burden ye must endure in order to be of understanding of others. Jesus needs to visit with ye tonight concerning Rebecca and Elizabeth. Read the first two chapters of Luke in preparation."

Jesus appeared to Mule on earth and spoke: "I know you are probably surprised to see me, but I forgot to tell you something: All things are possible if you believe hard enough. When you feel stronger, go get some tests done, but don't get discouraged and don't believe everything they say. Because if you want something bad enough, and you ask me, and I think it's right, then I'll let you have it. The doctors try to do a good job—but sometimes they don't quite make it.

"Remember Elizabeth: She was very sad, but I gave her a child even though she was old. It was a loving miracle I did for her. I won't tell you the future, because that would spoil everything.

"I know your head bothers you, and it has for years, but it was so important to keep you awake that anything was okay. Once a mule gets going you have to keep pushing her. The way you feel now will only last a day or so. I love you, and I didn't want you to fall asleep, but you'll be okay.

"I know your ears have been bad your whole life and always will be, but that doesn't mean I couldn't heal them if I wanted to. But it's best that everyone has one thing to deal with because it makes them more understanding of others. I didn't heal your ears completely, but I did give you back your hearing. Take care of them, and you'll be all right.

"I'm so happy. Just work on the pebbles, and don't get discouraged, because it's going to take a long time. Go in peace and get some sleep."

Albert spoke to Mule, "Be assured when the time comes, I will tell you what he is to be called."

Mule said, "Who, Albert?"

Albert said, "That of a child firstborn."

"But, Albert, I am not even married yet," Mule said. "And anyway, the doctors say I can't have a child."

Albert said, "Blessed be the man who fathers a child of miracles. A man of honor be entitled this, for ye shall not join hands with one unworthy."

I said, "Albert, Jesus strongly suggested that Mule would have a child, yet it barely penetrated her mulish head. Does she exhaust you as much as she does me?"

Albert said, "'Tis most pleasing with which I hear the simple eloquence that rolls forth from ye lips in understanding."

August 20, 1984

Jesus appeared to Mule on earth and spoke: "You're not dreaming; I'm really here. It hurt me to make you see all those things that hurt you. We had to push as fast as we could. I strengthened you greatly, but now you need to rest.

"Don't worry about your weight; you will be able to exercise all you want later. You worry about such unimportant things. You push yourself too hard. You try so hard to be perfect; why don't you just slow down and do what you can? If you don't rest, you'll collapse eventually. I'll see you soon."

When Jesus departed, Mule said, "Albert, Jesus sure does take good care of me."

Albert said, "Jesus walked through many pastures, be the flowers as of people: for as he loved his lambs and sheep, he beheld the flowers of much importance; for not only were they beautiful when they blossomed, he was of much pride. Many pastures did he walk and many flowers did he care for, for his hands touched them with much grace and upward they would sprout. Even in the desert, he felt each grain of sand: as it sifted down between his toes, it was transformed to glisten in the sunlight; thus barren, the desert was not."

Part VI

Modus Operandi

(August and September 1984)

You need to understand that we make you rest because we have things to show you. You can't build a new house on a tired foundation.

– Katrina

Chapter 28

Spiritual Paths

Albert speaks to Mule: "It matters not which path ye choose when there be a split in the woods: For as long as they both be smooth, they shall end in the same place. It just so happens some people a detour do take, and some people prefer a route of more directness. As long as ye know to where the path shall lead, and observe all the wonders along the way, eternal joy be assured."

Katrina escorts the essence of Mule's soul to the outskirts of Heaven, where they gaze upon a network of winding, intertwining paths.

Katrina says: "These are spiritual paths, and they all lead to God if you remember to call on Jesus. You have to keep these paths clear, just like the paths on earth. The paths are all different: some are rough, others smooth; some meander, others are straight; some are short, others long; some are dark, others light. Here is what your path looked like before you got some help." Mule's mighty rock blocks Heaven's Holy Light, casting the darkest of shadows on her path.

Katrina continues, "Every time you don't do what we (holy angels) say, you build a rock, and that's not right. Here is what your path looks like now that you have gotten some help."

Mule's rock has now broken into smaller chunks allowing a dim, dusky light onto the path. Mule walks hand in hand with Katrina down the path and notices that each chunk of rock has an attached label. Each label contains a written summary of a traumatic event in Mule's life; every trauma has been recorded.

Katrina says, "Once you examine each rock and accept the circumstances behind it, the rock will dissolve into the path. Don't ever be afraid and just throw them aside, or you will just build another pile. When you are scared, ask Jesus to help, and when you are sad, share it with someone—or another rock will form. To move a rock, you must identify the circumstances as being real, and then they will dissolve. The more you look at them, the more they will dissolve into the path."

Mule sees the rock marked "Luther."

Katrina says, "Luther is gone now, but there is a lot to learn from his memory—so don't just forget because you don't want to remember. He joined you when you were four years old and grew up with you. Why do you think he hated to go so much? He also invited a lot of his friends in at times, and many of these were at the Evil Party."

Mule glances to the side and sees Farmer's spiritual path running parallel with her own. The path is abundant with Holy Light, and no rocks block the way. Jesus and Farmer walk hand in hand along the path, with Lucinda following several paces behind. Jesus' animated gestures give the impression he is instructing Farmer on some important matters.

Mule looks to Katrina and says, "Can I go over there with Jesus?"

Katrina says, "You can't walk on another person's path, because each person's path is just for them and Jesus and nobody else. Farmer has a lot on his mind, and Jesus is going to help him now. Between Carla and you, the poor man has his hands full. Jesus is going to help settle his mind."

Katrina then escorts Mule to Heaven's Lake where they sit side by side on the grassy shore. Katrina says, "You need to understand that we make you rest because we have things to show you. You can't build a new house on a tired foundation."

Mule says, "Katrina, the lake is so beautiful."

Katrina says, "The more you believe, the prettier it gets."

Mule says, "Oh, look, Katrina! There's a deer over there."

Katrina says, "Yes, animals are God's creatures, so they get to go to Heaven. No animal will hurt you here. And tell Carla not to worry, because the dogs get to go to Heaven too. There's lots of room in Heaven for those who believe."

Mule surveys the distant horizon and sees a magnificent temple of gold with large, white doors at the entrance. She points to it and asks, "Can I go there, Katrina?"

Katrina says, "No, that's God's Throne Room, and it's not time for you to go there yet."

Mule asks, "Why don't I get to look as pretty as you?"

Katrina laughs and says, "Because I'm an angel, silly. But when you come to Heaven permanently, you'll be beautiful like an angel, because everything is beautiful in Heaven, just like Jesus told you.

"When you return, tell Farmer to go through your medicine cabinet with you and throw away all the drugs, because you need to feel the pain. Satan wanted you really badly; but in a spiritual sense, you can move things on your path that make you stumble. Everyone's path is different, but all paths lead to Heaven if you remember to call on Jesus."

Mule says, "Katrina, can I go to the Garden while I am here?"

Katrina says, "No. Jesus holds special talks in the Garden, and we can't go there right now. But we will show you more later if you just slow down and cooperate. We make you rest because we have things to show you, so stop resisting the sleep that comes upon you."

Chapter 29

Luther's Way

Albert speaks to Mule: "Be it known that ye are but advised to seek the truth neath the pebble marked 'Luther': for 'tis there that the beginning of the most fretful of darkness sprouted in an earthly time of long ago, which developed into depths as the spirit grew. Thus intertwining of darkness and evil grow hand in hand, for they cannot grow independent of each other."

Mule falls into a deep sleep and meets Katrina who says: "Remember: Luther is gone for good and cannot hurt you anymore. What happened was not your fault, but was because there was no talk of God in the house."

Mule sees a vision of herself as a four-year-old child, sleeping soundly in her childhood home. As she sleeps, Luther approaches her through a dream. He rides a camel covered with sparkling jewels. Luther is about the same size as Mule, and he wears a black, hooded monk's robe that totally obscures his hideous features. The strange sight captivates Mule.

Luther asks Mule, "Want to ride on my camel, my dear?"

Mule says, "I can't see you with your robe on."

Luther says, "I know, but I don't like all the light inside you."

Mule says, "Who are you?"

Luther says, "Well, you know that everyone has a spirit, and I'm your spirit."

With youthful innocence, Mule says, "Oh, thank you. But please tell me your name, so I'll know what to call you."

"No," Luther says. "My name is a secret. Secrets are a lot of fun, so it's best for us to have a lot of secrets."

Luther says, "You're lonely, aren't you, little girl?"

Mule replies with great sadness, "Yes, I am. Nobody likes me."

Luther says, "Well, I'll be your friend. You know, I like to play with little girls; and you're so innocent, I will really enjoy playing with you. Over the years, I've played with a lot of little girls, and you'll get to meet them someday."

Mule says, "That would be nice."

Luther says, "My dear, do you know what your imagination is?"

Mule says, "No, because that is a big word."

Luther says, "Well, it's just like the Sandman, the Tooth Fairy, and Santa: They are not real, you just think they are. That's your imagination. If you ever tell anyone about me, they'll just tell you that it's your imagination."

Mule says, "But you *are* real."

Luther says, "Of course, I am, my dear. But if you tell anyone, they won't believe you. My father has spent many years weaving that web."

Mule says, "Won't you be my friend anyway?"

Luther says, "Yes, little girl, I'll be your friend. I'll even live with you so you don't have to be lonely anymore. But first, I'll have to do a lot of work on you. I can't live in you right now, because there is some light inside of you that I don't like. Your heart is too light, but I'll just put up some curtains on my side and do some work. The first thing that I'll have to do, though, is to work on your thoughts.

"In the daytime, I'll play with you in your imagination. I'll work on making it dark inside of you and bring in some more friends later. But you must never tell anyone I am here, or I'll have to punish you."

Mule says, "Please don't punish me."

"Well, perhaps it won't be necessary," Luther says, "but here is someone you will definitely have to avoid."

Mule then sees a vision of Jesus with little children sitting on his lap. Luther says: "Jesus is a mean man, and his secret was that he really didn't like people. That's the way it is in real life too: everybody hates everybody, and they only pretend to like other people."

Mule then sees a vision of Jesus feeding people bread and fish (the actual event as described in the Bible). Luther says: "Jesus didn't really feed people bread and fish, because he didn't care about them; he only wanted to show them some magic tricks for his own fun. Everybody really hated Jesus because he was a bad man. Why else do you think they killed him? So the lesson is that it's bad to love people, because it's just a game, just like it was with Jesus."

Mule says, "What is love?"

Luther cackles with glee and says: "Well, if you don't know what love is, I'm certainly not going to be the one to tell you. If you let yourself care about other people, it hurts—and you don't want to hurt, do you? If you ever let yourself care about other people, I'm going to kill them or make them go away. If you even try to love other people, I'm going to make it hurt you. You know, it's best to never get started loving other people, because it always ends up hurting. As soon as you think you understand what love is, and it doesn't confuse you anymore, you're in a lot of trouble. Be faithful only to me, or you'll pay."

Mule says, "Will you play with me, then, so I won't be all alone?"

Luther says: "Of course, I will. I have lots of games. I love games."

Mule asks, "What kind of games?"

Luther says: "There is a great game for you to play that takes the place of caring about other people: Just sit alone in a corner and stare off into space and rock back and forth. It's just like pulling a curtain around you so you can't feel. Humans sometimes call it autism."

Mule says, "That's a very funny name."

Luther says, "Yes, funny name and funny game."

Luther continues: "No one will believe you if you tell them about me. We can be together forever. I'll never go away from you, but I might have to punish you if you're mean to me. You belong only to me now. Yes, I believe with some hard work, we can block off the light around your heart so that I will be more comfortable in here. That will be no problem."

As the vision continues, Mule sees numerous traumas in her life and how Luther is behind most of them. She does not know that Luther is causing her problems at the time, as he does not allow himself to enter her conscious mind. Therefore, she blames all of her troubles on herself or others, causing many related problems.

Luther says: "When you got older, you were harder to handle, so I brought in some friends to help control you. You were so much easier to play with when you were younger. My father, Satan, told me to bring some of the rocks of Hell to pack around your heart to keep you from feeling."

Luther packs a bucket of rocks and ashes around Mule's heart. He screams, "I don't want you to feel, but that's okay, because nobody can break through these rocks!"

Luther moves from Mule's heart to her brain. The Demon of Lust joins him. They both examine the intricate network of cobwebs woven throughout.

Luther asks Lust, "How do you like my toy?"

"Oh, she is just perfect, Luther," Lust says with hysteric glee. "What a confusing web you've woven in her mind. Nothing can penetrate that web."

Luther says: "Yes, but she is so hard to handle. My father said that I could do anything I wanted with her, but you have to help me play with her in order to control her."

Luther turns to Mule and says, "As you got older and started trying to figure out what was wrong, I didn't know what to do with you. I had done such a good job with you that I thought it was time for you to go see my father."

In the background, Mule hears Luther's children taunting: "Mule, come out and play; Mule, come out and play in the dark."

Luther sneers and says: "The wicked man is such a fool to give you medicine for hearing voices. Voices can come from Above or voices can come from Below, but they are certainly real. It is so obvious. Oh, well, humans are stupid, and they will never learn."

Luther becomes angry at Mule for trying to get help. "I'm going to visit my father and tell on you, because I want to please him. He wants you real bad. You're not going to get any help from the wicked man."

Mule says, "But I feel so bad, I need somebody to help me."

Luther snarls and says: "I want you all for my own. I'll never let you have a family or a child, because I won't share you with anybody. Anyway, you can't love, so it will never be a problem. Believe me, I have my ways, and I'll get you to kill yourself soon. Then you can come with me forever. If you keep reaching for help, I'm going to hurt you, and then you'll learn. Don't listen to anything that wicked man tells you."

When Farmer gives Mule the cross necklace in January of 1984, Mule sees the cobwebs in her mind dissolving.

Luther shouts at Mule: "I don't want anything to go into your mind about God, because then it can go into your heart.

You should never accept anything from another person, especially something like a cross. Everything the wicked man is telling you about Jesus is wrong. You deserve all the pain you are going through, because you are bad. You are so bad that Jesus will never love you. I'm going to tell my father about you now."

Mule sees Luther arrive at Satan's throne room in the core of Hell. The throne room is like a deep rock cave, full of darkness and smoke. Satan is very angry about the course of events and provides Luther with more rocks to pack around Mule's heart. He also provides a contingent of demonic reinforcements to help control her and to dissuade Farmer from helping her further.

Upon Luther's return, he places suicidal thoughts into Mule's mind. When Farmer considers hospitalization for Mule, Luther rants at her, "People will do bad things to you at the hospital, so you should be afraid to go there for help. They will never let you out of there; you will die there."

When it becomes clear that Mule is going to the hospital, Luther warns her, "Don't like the people there, because they will go away and it will hurt."

Mule sees Luther causing her intense emotional and physical pain in the hospital, especially when others express care or talk with her about God. He kneads and twists her intestines to punish her. The physicians at the hospital have no idea what they are dealing with, and this delights Luther.

When Mule encounters the hospital chaplain, the cobwebs in her mind break up further. The holy angels prompt her to ask the chaplain if there really is a devil. The chaplain answers affirmatively. As the chaplain prays for her, Luther is enraged because the cobwebs continue to fall away.

Luther returns to Hell to consult with Satan. Satan provides him with a host of demonic guards. The guards are assigned to prevent Mule from hearing more about God and to aid Luther in subduing Farmer during direct confrontations.

Luther speaks to Mule, "They cannot have you, because you are my toy." Mule sees the gathering demonic forces preparing for battle.

Mule then sees many of the confrontations between Farmer and the forces of evil occurring in June 1984. Luther laughs uncontrollably at Farmer's belief that he might be gone for good. Luther hopes to set Farmer up to be killed when his guard is down.

In early July 1984, the angels of God come inside Mule's mind and take up positions against the demons. Luther senses he is in big trouble. The Holy Light surrounding the angels further disintegrates Luther's sticky web.

Luther screams at Mule, "How could you do this to me? Damn you, now you've gotten these angels in here. I'm going to go tell my father."

Luther returns from consulting Satan and is filled with the false hope of ultimate victory. He scolds Mule, "I've been here a long time, and since you're so hard to play with, I can make you four again." Mule then sees the July 4, 1984, regression.

The vision ends with a review of the final two battles with Luther on July 7, 1984.

Chapter 30

Lustful Perversions

Katrina speaks to Mule: "The work you are doing is important and going well, even though you may be tired of contending with the demons. Sometimes these things are allowed to happen to strengthen you, and once you get to the other side, you appreciate it more. When you are in this situation, you don't see the progress, but it is going real well.

"I have something to show you now so you will understand; it's not good to hide it away. I'll hold your hand so it won't hurt so much."

As the vision begins, the twenty-year-old Mule attends a party. The Demon of Lust deceptively subdues her soul, takes possession of her body, and makes sexual advances towards a man of Lust's choosing. Mule has no idea what has come over her; she consciously resists Lust's impulses, but they are too overwhelming. One thing leads to another, and the couple ends up having sex in an upstairs bedroom.

Mule relives the shame and humiliation she felt at the time, believing that she alone was responsible for her behavior. Lust laughs at Mule as it departs the scene.

Luther arrives and laughs at Lust's trick. However, when he realizes that Mule is pregnant, the joke ends. The thought of sharing Mule with a child makes him insanely jealous. Luther is determined to destroy the newly conceived child before Mule discovers the pregnancy.

Katrina says to Mule: "Luther was angry because he thought you might want to keep the baby, and he was too jealous to let that happen. Luther was so stupid he didn't understand that he was seeking to destroy one of his own, a creation of evil."

As Luther savagely beats the newly conceived child to death, he yells, "You'll never take her away from me!"

Katrina says to Mule: "Luther was allowed to destroy the baby, because the situation was prompted by the Demon of Lust. It's okay for it to hurt, but remember—blessings sometimes come in disguised ways." Katrina adds, "There is something else that you need to understand."

As the vision continues, Mule unknowingly befriends a man who belongs to Satan. The Demon of Lust possesses Mule and the Demon of Violence possesses the man; their interplay results in the man sexually assaulting Mule. Physicians say this assault will prevent Mule from ever having a child.

Lust says to Mule: "I made that happen while you were being good so you would be afraid to be close to anyone again. Only a little tramp would allow herself to be used like that. Jesus can't possibly love you when you've committed the worst sin of all.

"I can make you do the same things with the wicked man. I'll get even with him, because I can tempt anybody. It will be a cinch to tempt him and turn him away from Jesus, because everybody can be tempted."

As the vision continues, Mule sees Lust's August 8, 1984, attack against the Farmer.

Lust's narration continues: "You know, it's really no big deal anyway, because everybody commits sexual sin; they just try to twist it in their own minds to justify it. Those who do it all the time outside of God's blessing will never be loved by him. I'm going to be ready for the (evil) party, but first I'm going to make you do some things you'll regret, and that will destroy your progress for a while."

Lust then possesses Mule and tries to prompt her into evil. Fortunately, however, the holy angels prevent Mule from leaving home by giving her an overwhelming urge to sleep.

Lust says to Mule: "You think you're so innocent, but you're not. You are a cheap little sleaze just like all other women. After I get the wicked man to sin at the party, then no one will love him either."

Mule then sees a replay of the Evil Party. At the end of the party, Katrina and Lucinda arrive to escort Lust away.

Lust says to Mule: "You'll remember me, because I wove a web just like Luther did—only I didn't weave it in your mind, I wove it in your desires. You'll never sort that out, because you're so confused anyway, and your mother helped me out by giving you a lot of guilt about these things. You'll never forget me, because I left something behind, and I'll cross your path again."

Lust says to Katrina and Lucinda: "You angels just don't know what you are missing by not having sex." The holy angels laugh at Lust as they escort it away.

Upon completion of the vision, Mule tells Farmer what has occurred, and he transcribes it. The forces of evil then savagely choke Mule.

After the attack is repelled, Albert says: "When a valued secret be told of them for the purpose of using the knowledge in aiding others, there be that of revenge: for evil likes man not to know their secret ways. Be assured their harsh violence shall come no more.

"They choke ye, for they like not that of the truth spoken. The hand of their father be most cruel, but shall not overcome against those of the Lord. Alas, also be it of memory the warning of trouble when in search of the dark secrets of the evil ones. They despise the thought of men knowing their evil methods."

Chapter 31

The Demon Guards

Albert speaks to Farmer: "Alas, for I have found the demon guards who were in flee of the light. They have nested high upon the bluffs of reason and judgment. Behold, I tell ye that a great net has been cast upon them by the guards thus binding them of their performance and making ready for spaces of improvements. It is of great difficulty to deliver my discovery for these very circumstances. A mule is of delight when standing still, yet how may he move if his hooves be bound to the ground?

"The one with the ear of value is but unknowingly misled into thoughts of revolt, but this be of the guards and not the soul. There be two guards, each of which may be forced to go when the knots of the mighty rope be severed. They crouch there in seclusion of deep grayness, yet I may not dispose of them unless the word is sent to me from the Mighty One, and *only* Jesus. Recall the words of authority sent, and be it known that light smashes darkness into harmless grains.

"This be an extermination of most importance, for it chains down the plow of progress, thus hindering the planting time.

A log has dammed the river so it must be set to the side: for if the river were to overrun the banks, the waters would prove to be most destructive. Administer to the guards as in ye would to the pagans among nature. When the river flows and the slumber comes, they shall be washed away with the grains."

As the vision begins, Mule sees the inside of her brain. Each brain structure is labeled according to its function.

Two demon guards, shaped like giant, dark clouds, approach from the distance. The demon guards carry a thick net that they place over the brain structures labeled "judgment" and "reason." The net prevents Mule from exercising her judgment and reason faculties, resulting in many mishaps that greatly slow her progress.

Katrina appears within Mule's brain, and Mule says, "Katrina, I am scared that the guards are going to hurt me."

Katrina says: "Ask for help from Jesus, and then wait on the Lord and be of good courage; and then you don't have to be afraid. The more you hold back from asking for help, the deeper the soil for the Demon of Depression. You have to start caring for people in a real way to fight this demon."

Mule says, "What can I do about the guards?"

Katrina says: "It's real important to pray. If you need help to pray, ask Jesus first, ask for one of the angels, read your Psalms, or ask another person to help you. Don't be afraid to ask for help to pray now. Later, you won't need anyone's help to pray."

Lucinda, endowed with an extra measure of Holy Light, arrives within Mule's brain and places the Holy Light on the cowering demon guards, causing them to disintegrate. Albert and Katrina then remove the net blocking Mule's judgment and reason. The net, like the guards, disintegrates.

Katrina says to Mule: "The thought you had earlier that God was punishing you was from the guards. You know God would never punish you. It was not a smart thing to forget to wear your cross; the guards didn't want you to, but you could have if you had tried harder. It's real important to know about the guards, because they can be influencing you without you having any idea about it. I'm glad to help you with these things if you just ask.

"Please don't be angry about all the time this is taking from your work, because it is necessary, or it wouldn't have worked out that way. There will be time for visiting your family later, so it's not important."

Albert and Farmer join Mule within the confines of her brain. Farmer says, "Albert, why are these demons called guards?"

Albert says, "They be distinguished by their function, for what is blocked is displayed in the action of the personality. Be it known that they may access the intelligence and personality of anyone."

Farmer says, "They also prevent people from hearing God's word, don't they, Albert?"

Albert says: "Yes, for 'tis much like that of placing a fence around a soul, limiting the reach of choice: thus the conscious mind comprehends not that of the curtain drawn."

Albert says to Mule: "When ye have suspicions, even but in the smallest of doubt, 'tis wise to seek assistance and pray in hands: For guards bearing despair seek pleasure in roosting over embers of hope. It be of great importance to be fooled not by those voices of ye mind which say 'tis not necessary to seek help, for 'tis a deceptive disguise. Hopelessness be of torment on the mind by Satan's wand: thus resist greatly, for God's children never be of hopelessness."

Chapter 32

Katrina's Review

Katrina escorts the essence of Mule's soul to the lake in Heaven and says: "You have worked hard to look at the pebbles so that the foundation can be laid, or as Albert says, 'the rows be planted.' It would be good to review the visions to help with understanding. The field is half patted down now, and that's real good. During the winter months will be the time to take root.

"Just remember to pray, and stop worrying about time. A few months out of a lifetime isn't really much—and compared to eternity, it isn't even a grain. Rest to restore your strength because the work will have to continue until it is finished.

"You may get frustrated because Farmer makes you go over things, but it is necessary for things to be understood, forgiven, and forgotten. Then your heart has room for other things. You need to learn how to care, and we'll teach you how with little projects.

"Everything is going really well, and although you may have felt pushed, what has happened over the last few months would have taken years if we hadn't. It was important to move fast to prevent more evil from coming back to a greater degree. The demons are so ugly in nature, aren't they?

"You talk about being discouraged, but please try not to be by believing the outcome is well worth the work. Stop being frustrated about things getting back to normal. It really isn't necessary to worry about such things. The work you and the good doctor are doing is far more important.

"The only demon still in residence of your soul is the Demon of Depression, which has been with you as long as Luther, and that is why it is so hard for you to tell the difference when it is around. Go fast on understanding so it won't sneak by. You get discouraged so easily at times; you'll have to get over that. After the Demon of Depression is removed, you will be able to identify discouragement freely and act accordingly.

"Tell Farmer not to worry about his techniques when dealing with the demons; you both learn best by doing. He is extremely wise to Albert's instructions and doing exceptionally well.

"When Farmer writes his book, we're all going to help him if he asks. Also, when he writes, there may be some attacks because the demons won't like it. But don't be afraid, for you know what to do—and obviously, so does he.

"Just because Albert doesn't talk to you as much doesn't mean he's gone away, so don't panic. But his main function of giving instructions has been largely fulfilled. Many sick and blind people need to hear his lyre, and that is where he is at times, because that work is worthwhile too.

"It's true that all will be well when the cherry blossoms fall. When instructions for celebration are given in the spring, Albert will let you know what to do."

Part VII

The Cherry Blossoms

(September 1984 – March 1985)

'Tis most true that all shall be well when the cherry blossoms fall, for then it shall be spring.

– Albert

Chapter 33

The Working of the Land

Albert instructed Mule: "'Tis a gleam in the eye of the Master, for the projects be underway. Be assured he has a most pleasing smile.

"Now 'tis time to focus on that of inspecting pebbles until they dissolve into the path. Ye have been given all of the components with which to work, for the scenes evolved of rock-moving most certainly fell from the rock into pebble form. After one has viewed many scenes in an intense fashion, it be best to go back and examine each with that of the same intensity: for once the past has been but inspected and understood, then that of building upon the foundation in an upward direction be possible with strength. Review and reflect as in discussions like those of critiques. Words of knowledge be not always necessary when the pebbles lie at ye feet.

"'Tis of great importance to understand events as they were, forgive, and thus let the past crumble into dust—not so as to be forgotten, for dust may become astir in a breeze or scuffle, but so as to be not in the way of the future with its pebbles as obstacles to walk upon daily. After one has been freed from a classroom of darkness, learning starts anew; but, oh, how swift and joyous it is when the Blessed Teacher is in command, for he will not let you falter needlessly."

Mule asked, "Albert, why am I so tired?"

Albert said: "Ye have been weakened of strength, for those who can go not a'wandering must spend restful time renewing and listening. False strength be like that of false pride, so be thee wise, for ye shall receive words of ready. Also, a lesson is at hand and that be one of patience, for 'tis better to accept and adapt than to resist and ruin. A mule could transport a sizeable load if he worried less about how far the journey."

Mule said, "But I feel better now."

Albert said: "'Tis best to think of ye body as a home overrun by vagrants for many a year; thus intense trauma and destruction has been endured through illness and stress, housing occupants of vile natures. So as a light dusting of rest scatters upon ye, be it not mistaken for that of true energy: for 'tis a false cloak enveloping weary tissues, portraying itself as fitness by the deceptions of the wicked.

"Be not like the runner of eager anxiety at the blocks, for he only delays that of the race with many a false start. It matters not how tightly the reins be held on ye; for control of falsely surging currents be most necessary or ye shall collapse, hence falling prey to the wicked. Ye shall be advised as to the time repairs are complete. 'Tis best not to think far into the months, but only of the time at hand. A snug harness be of loving discipline, for to be under control is of great importance for a steady recovery.

"It has been told from Above that ye be of a fragile nature, thus 'tis wise to let not that of an occasional passerby break ye nature like that of a dry twig: For a soul that receives nurturing through prayer and faith shall never be destroyed, as those be the basics that thus provide pliability for which to withstand all weather and influences of the darkness. Hence a bending twig in need of support must accept the stake when 'tis provided, for

THE WORKING OF THE LAND   183

there be no shame in reaching forth when in need of an anchor at a time of unsteady leg. 'Tis best to keep in mind, all things which take root be shaky in the time of wee hours, yet behold how tall and sturdy the mighty redwood stands."

Mule asked, "Why haven't you told the Farmer to loosen the reins?"

Albert replied, "A firm hand be most necessary, for the Farmer may do as he wishes."

Mule said, "But things aren't like they used to be."

Albert explained: "Ye be most correct in knowing the perils of the past are much like that of water over the dam, yet 'tis with great concern that I make ye mindful that the destination to the opposite shore is not yet of completion. To be in watchful eye as told from Above be not a punishment like those neath the bars of formal correction, for there be few who reside upon the earth who know well the sly ways of wicked neighbors. With endless hours of idle time, a guiding hand is of much benefit: for one who seeks shelter neath a blanket of solitude may open an eye not of his own vision."

Mule protested, "I appreciate everything being done for me, but please ask Jesus why I can't at least have some time to do other things."

Albert said: "Jesus knows well the tenderness of ye heart and desires to help, yet he is also of great knowledge of ye mule-like thinking which at times contains no logic; thus it is said to ye to rest, for many a year of conflicting struggles have resided within ye soul. Time for the deed has been appointed ye, for to buck and burrow ye heels neath that of the soil only is of a prolonging nature. Upon the newness of the week, if ye have displayed obedience to the Farmer's commands as influenced by the Master, then ye be of a deserving nature to have selected spans of time in which to test the stability of ye legs."

Mule asked, "Why has it taken this long for the demons to be disposed of?"

Albert said: "When the Farmer begins to build that of a windmill to thus supply power from waving currents of wind, he is able not to construct it in a day of a few hours, as there are many small parts which thus act as the center core for strength of the structure. If he were to abandon labor when having only two blades built for he noticed it turned neath the fingertips of the breeze, he would note with much sadness after that of a heavy storm the mill would stand no more, and he would thus have to set out once more on labor of many hours. Yet if he builds in faith and rests after times of strain for his mighty hands, he thus stands back and views a mill of great beauty capable of harnessing winds of harshness in all types of weather. Therefore, is it not better to build through three seasons of a structure which shall stand for a lifetime than to hurry beckoned by impatience only to build again?

"Be it also much like this: A man with many idle hours leaves his mind open like a well of which he could drown in by unsuspecting thoughts. After the days of celebration have passed and ye be of a stronger health, ye may occasionally be away from the orchard of supervision only as the orchard keeper sees fit, for he be of a much wiser mind than ye. Rejoice in knowing that the mud be not as deep as past seasons, and thus contemplate on the bounty of the spring, not the gloominess of now."

Mule asked, "Will the demons all be gone by springtime?"

Albert replied: "'Tis most true that all shall be well when the cherry blossoms fall, for then it shall be spring. Hence as it is with all things of nature in the birth of spring, 'tis a time to welcome newness of sprouts and buds which burst forth into colors of beauty and harvests of plenty. As it is with a season of late planting, the seeds need be in the soil by that of the time when the apple leaves drift downward from the limbs to light upon the ground as a blanket, thus protecting it from the cold.

"When the heaviness of labor be done and the furrows patted snugly to make ready for the embracing flakes of winter,

THE WORKING OF THE LAND   185

then there be time to sit at the loom of common bothers and reaching for strands of care to intertwine, thus forcing assured destruction of the lowly worm (Demon of Depression). Once the field be planted and tucked in for the nap of winter, fewer explorers shall pass by, for it is but done and firmly sealed. With the welcoming of the spring, the Farmer shall behold the beauty of his labors and share in joy with the Mule, for without each other the bountiful crops would be not. Be there many reasons to share in that of festive joy."

Mule said: "But, Albert, we have already worked so hard for so long. We have finally moved the rock and viewed the pebbles; but now we have to plow the field, plant the seeds, and nurture the sprouts. This is all too much. Why doesn't God just snap his fingers and make everything perfect?"

With a hint of weariness, Albert said: "This turmoil has been but composed over the changing seasons for many years, thus how foolish to expect in that of an instant to evict all evil inhabitants and make the path smooth."

Mule said, "The wait seems endless."

Albert said: "Be thee not discouraged, for the working of the land is the most tedious of chores; yet the bountiful harvest that is assured shall perish thoughts of how weary ye bones and how long the hours in ye mind: For if a man had been of crippled leg for many a year and thus came of knowledge that he may walk with that of constant exercising in good faith—though he may not be able to walk by that of week's end—he shall run freely one day abounding in joy and hold it happily in his heart he quit not his efforts when overcome by that of despair. As he skips merrily along, he will think back upon the dust of the path and remember not the intense pain and hardship, but be so thankful it may have been; for those who labor intensely be of more enjoyment of their efforts, for they know the true and earnest value of what they have. This be so more of spiritual value which is priceless as compared to those things of material possessions that shall be nonexistent in the Land of the Fadeless Day."

Mule said, "I don't think Farmer will be able to tolerate me until the time of the cherry blossoms."

Albert said, "Just as the Mule needs the Farmer to guide it and tend to its needs, the Farmer needs the Mule to aid in the turning of the soil of knowledge so he can create a crop of understanding which will reap plentiful salvation for mankind. At times, coordination of the wills be more difficult than the chores at hand, for neither one can accomplish the purpose of the goal alone: for it shall come to pass that if the Farmer cares for his Mule, and the Mule steadily obeys his commands, a crop of glory unlike any other shall be absorbed into the minds and souls of men."

Chapter 34

Day of the Cherry Blossoms

March 17, 1985

"Albert," I said, "are there any demons trespassing on Mule's field?"

"No, for all is well in the bird's nest." The weak answer revealed the counterfeiter, but I didn't tip my hand.

I said, "Albert, so I can be sure it is you, verify the name of my mother's guardian angel."

After a pause, the counterfeiter said, "Tamara."

I said, "Did you mean to say Tasia? What about her other guardian, Luticia?"

The counterfeiter paused again. Then, most surprisingly, he began to cry.

I said, "Come forth, demon. What's your name?"

The demon said, "My name is Simon. Please don't hurt me; I promise I won't hurt her." I suspected a demonic ruse, but the Holy Spirit told me that Simon was filled with genuine sadness and no threat to Mule.

I said: "Simon, I do not allow anyone to trespass on Mule's field. You must go."

Simon cried even more intensely. He said: "I want to go home. Satan sent me here, so I had to come. Satan is mean and wants to kill her, but I promise I won't hurt her. I just don't know what to do."

I said, "Jesus, please surround us with a cocoon of silence so that Simon's words cannot be heard by Satan. Also, please remove any knowledge of what was said previously."

Jesus said, "Wait for a moment." After about a minute, Jesus said, "You may proceed when ready."

I asked, "What exactly do you want me to do, Simon?"

Simon sobbed: "Please help me go back home. I don't like Satan. He lured me from Heaven with the promise that I could hand out love-flowers in a beautiful land called Hell. He lied to me. Now, I just want to go home. I don't want to hurt her. I just don't know what to do. Please help me."

I said, "Simon, I am not in the habit of helping fallen angels, but I have compassion for your plight. You seem of sincere heart. The only thing you *can* do is to pray to God to let you go back. It's his decision. There is no one else you can turn to. So that is my suggestion: pray hard to God to go back home, and see what happens."

Simon smiled through his tears and said, "Thank you. You are not a wicked man like Satan says."

I said, "Simon, you must go now. I will ask that the cocoon of silence be removed, and then I will dispatch you in such a way that no evil will suspect your intentions."

Simon said, "Thank you. I understand."

Jesus then removed the cocoon of silence, and I sternly said to Simon, "In the name of Jesus, go where Jesus wishes you to go, but do not trespass on this field ever again."

Albert said: "For those most sorrowfully deceived, they learn the error of their ways, yet at times, 'tis too late: for they fell to the Master of Lies and would only have a subsequent attempt to gain the Lord's favor and reenter the Kingdom with a most continual prayer, not to reach Satan's ears, but loudly in the soul. And perhaps if the sincerity is of a most pure truth, they may be allowed back."

I said, "Albert, that was a poor attempt by Simon to counterfeit you."

Albert said, " 'Twas a kumquat on a pear tree: for he would have liked to stay and make a nest in a home of a safe tree, yet he was tormented by his tears."

I said, "The tears were genuine, weren't they?"

Albert said, "They be of much heavy sadness like that of the tears of a cloud on a day of no sun, as if weeping for the loss of a belief most dear."

I asked, "He really didn't want to hurt Mule, did he?"

Albert said, "It crushed him much, for 'tis much like the humane to be required to crush the skull of an innocent pup."

I asked, "Where does Simon go now?"

Albert said, "Through the sincerity of his desires, he may thus be lifted up gradually to skim the surface and perhaps ascend to his home once more if his prayers be deep."

March 21, 1985

Some demon was trespassing on Mule's field, and I was going to punish him well. "Come forth, demon," I said. To my surprise, it was Simon who came forth.

Simon said: "Please don't be mad at me. I won't hurt her. I just wanted to tell you something."

Simon was filled with love and joy abounding, radiant with the Holy Spirit.

I said, "What do you want to tell me, Simon?"

Simon said: "The Lord God said that because I was sorry for my mistake and of sincere heart, I could return to the Garden in Heaven. God said never to listen to Satan again. I am on my way home now, but I just wanted to tell you and thank you for helping me."

I said, "How happy I am for you, Simon, holy angel of God. Your story will be told throughout eternity as a testament to your faith. Peace be with you."

Simon smiled, lightly touched my hand, and said, "And peace be unto the Farmer of men's souls." He then joyously departed for Heaven.

Albert said: "It takes a free hand to lift a glass in toast of celebration. Be he a lily of white once again, for his repentance and prayer was most fervent; thus he be humming in the Garden once again, as he dusts the petals of the flowers and feeds them with love."

March 25, 1985

The long-awaited day of the cherry blossoms had finally arrived. In the preceding months, Mule and I had done battle with numerous demons: Samuel, Alice, Ernest, Lloyd, Sheba, Thomas, Essie, Samshiah, Frederick, the Demon of Depression, imps and guards, thugs and tormentors, named and generics, on and on. Yet after today, the forces of evil would be permanently weeded from Mule's soul.

Albert spoke to Mule: "Behold, for as the dawn rises, it shall burst into a blossom of a most glorious day. And though the winds may push a darkened cloud cross the sky, it shall not overrun the earth: for 'tis a fertile place of growing things of goodness. Thus the blossoms shall fall and shower the earth with praise."

Albert spoke to Farmer: "One may soon place his tools away in the barn, never to be to the degree of callused hand as has been the difficult work of late. Never be mindless of the contents in ye barn: for though ye may not need to hitch them to horse or hack away at the weeds, the tools of belief are best stored for ready access and are well cared for, as they are most priceless."

<hr>

"I'm going to kill her," the no-name demon threatened. "I'm going to kill her." The demon guided Mule's hands up to her own throat and squeezed with a death grip.

As I worked to counter the threat, the demon roared like a lion. The sound was so authentic, I expected to look around and see jungle foliage.

The demon spat, "She's going to lose, wicked man." By now, all demon threats rang hollow to my ears.

After the demon was finally dispatched, Albert said: "Angry vengeance is much like that of a wild animal seeking the ravages of raw meat, for they growl viciously and are not easy to let go of their prey. Thus it is done once, and twice remains to the ending where they shall rest in a sealed grave forever, not to stalk the grounds ever again."

<hr>

Alice, a female fallen angel, was the next foolish trespasser. "Alice," I commanded, "be gone in the name of Jesus."

"No, I don't have to," she petulantly replied.

I repeated the command.

"Why?" she asked. "Will you send me to Hell if I don't?"

The depth of her stupidity momentarily silenced me.

"You see," Alice explained, "I much prefer Hell to Heaven because the Dark Commander lives in Hell."

I said, "Jesus is the light."

Alice shot back, "The light is in the fire."

I shook my head with disgust and said, "You are a fine example of a female, Alice; you must be very proud."

She haughtily replied, "Well, I am much better than that vulgar angel, Lucinda. And Katrina, she is entirely too sweet for my tastes."

After much prayer, Alice's spirit was finally expelled from Mule's container. And then there was one left to go.

The demonic spirit deceitfully possessed Mule without my immediate notice. Suddenly, it propelled Mule's body towards the door in an attempt to escape the inevitable. I tackled Mule's body with gentle relish.

"You've lost demon," I exulted. "Jesus has defeated you."

The evil spirit cried out with a curious compulsion, "You're right; the Lord is God."

I commanded, "Repeat it, demon."

It repeated, "The Lord is God."

I forced the demon to repeat its concession again and again before dispatching it. As it departed, it squealed in torment, no doubt due in part to Satan's punishment for its words of surrender to the Lord.

Albert spoke to Mule: "The most magnificent splendor is in that of the greatest simplicity, thus it is so as in nature: for 'tis not at the mercy of man to be decoratively draped for awe. The greatest joy is in that of the worship and belief in the Lord; hence it is so that celebration among nature is a joyful blossom of pleasure and respect. Offer a psalm of praise in nature with the one who tightened ye harness with many a difficult tug, as he is known and favored for his mighty and devoted task."

Mule asked, "Albert, now that the cherry blossoms have fallen, are you going to leave us?"

Albert replied, "It reflects upon plans of the Master; yet at special times, visits are assured."

I said, "Mule and I will miss having you around as much, Albert."

Albert replied: "Yea, for when there is a twinkle in the heart, it is thus seen in the eye. Peace and love, noble one."

Chapter 35

The Farmer's Travail

Albert spoke to Farmer, fatigued by his many trials and difficult labor: "When the time arrives that a hardy hand has pulled many a mangled stump from the soil, it is of a great soreness; and thus the simple act of snapping one's fingers in joy becomes a motion of much pain. This be so from the condition of mighty work. Thus 'tis best to wash ye hands well and let them rest upon ye lap till joyful clapping abounds, absent in thought of joints of movement.

"Yet as it is in a cave, be it not with ye: for one who remains in the seclusion of darkness may be sensitive to the light, just as one remaining secluded in his thoughts loses the touch for others. Yet be at peace in the knowledge that your chores are well recognized in eyes of great proudness, for they be the eyes of the Father.

"Rescue ye mind from the depths of scholarly thinking so pensive in nature: for at times, ye be of a depth of thinking deeper than mines of coal. 'Tis well known ye will only be social at times, if absolutely necessary, for ye be most happy like that of the hermit neath the tree in thought. And though one would not expect a giraffe to live among igloos, some semblance of balance be healthy."

I said, "Have you been keeping up with the writings, Albert?"

Albert said: "One may assess in many ways that it be much like a boulder in a riverbed of pebbles. Ye expression be fabulous, with many facts and great truth—dramatic upon the points— the finest of grapes for the grandest of wines. Yet one would expect so from one so confidently selected in a task so heavy."

I said, "It's a lot of work."

Albert said, "'Tis a most tremendous sight to see the frost upon the leaves, even though the sun will erase the tracings."

I said, "Albert, have you noticed how the process of writing the book has flushed out evil spirits and evil people from every nook and cranny?"

Albert said: "Ones encamped around the burning fires of life shall only be scorched when attempting to extinguish it, for 'tis a roaring core of jubilance incapable of being smothered by little hands of wickedness. Thus 'tis best to add a stick at a time with great content."

I asked, "Do you know when the trials will be over?"

Albert said: "'Tis with eager heart I long to assist ye, for my fondness overwhelms me. Though I be of an unknown nature and a higher power to many who roam the earth, it sorrows my heart to not be given the information when addressed to the Master; yet the twinkle reflected in his eyes, much like the stars in the heavens, is most assuring of an umbilical outcome for ye, as the attachment is great. When the time arises for me to send forth the words, I shall not delay.

"Yet all is not barren like the desert lands: for though they have the appearance of being dry and mundane, after the drought has passed, many a bloom shall blossom upon the cactus. Thus worry not of brittle thorns to scratch upon ye during the day. See how the bird nesting upon the cactus enjoys the succulent juices, for he knows well his way around the thorns.

"Ye, Farmer, be much like the fowl known as the eagle: For it has the keenest of minds and claws of firmness which hold fast to branches without a waver of balance. Through the eyes of the eagle, the senses are sharpened, for it observes intricate detail and calculates well its moves; yet its wingspan commands the currents, for he knows to where he flies."

I said, "I'll do my best to make the mocking-birds see the truth, so that they might be saved."

Albert said, "Though the whippoorwill may be heard for many a mile, he sings of his own enjoyment while those caring not to hear are deaf to the matter—and though they may not open their hearts, they shall stumble around in solitude never knowing the joy of music. Also take note of the hummingbird: for he may sing whether perched upon a cactus top or resting upon a honeysuckle, as he knows the true source of light; thus he may even sing in the dark, as there is no despair in the light of truth to smother the songs of the heart."

Now, more than ever, I understood what the Mule had taught me: Jesus makes the birds sing.

Part VIII

Farmer's Conversations with Albert

"Albert, God obviously knew that I would ask many questions if I had access to an angel. But why did he choose one who speaks as complexly as you to answer?"

"To cultivate the fields of intelligence. And those who deem themselves to be great thinkers shall have much material to reflect upon."

"Should I paraphrase your responses for those who are less verbal?"

"The complexity of the originals be well put and thus be morsels for men thinking themselves of such profound intelligence."

– Farmer and Albert

Albert's Preface to the Conversations

As the captain and his first mate set sail upon the seas of human mysteries, they be in search of reverent waters flowing abundantly with those of spiritual currents containing answers. Many a turbulent storm tossed them about as precipitated by those of evil powers where the waters be the blackest; yet the mighty hand of the Lord anchored them safely in the bays of calmness, so times of reflection, thanksgiving, and navigation would be of a most restful value. Though the horizon be in sight and they must sail forth with joyous eyes upon it, 'tis best not to think of the distance, for it shall pass smoothly neath the power of the billowy sails rustling in a Divine breeze.

When the ship docks portside, many shall greet it with awe and admiration for the crew. A Handpicked crew be of special value, for not all would have the courage to endure such a journey of turbulence. Thus as a team be chosen for a journey, they shall also work best in casting out the net of knowledge, for both be not always at the same surface of the sea during the vile storms. 'Tis much the same as a captain sending a diver to the depths, only to pull him back once more and hear of the wonders that layeth neath the waters: together, they find the treasures.

Conversation 1

Soul and Holy Spirit

Spirit is that of the life of the eternal soul, just as the soul is the life of the earthly body.

– Albert

Albert spoke: "When the sun comes out to play in the early morning hours, it may smile at ye back so a shadow casts in front of ye. This is but a way it shows the image of ye self; hence take note how much larger the shadow becomes when the hours of the day dwindle down into the eve. This be so of ye soul as the years of life pass by."

"Albert, what exactly is a soul?"

"The soul is the body given the innermost essence of spirit."

"How do you define spirit?"

"Spirit is that of the life of the eternal soul, just as the soul is the life of the earthly body."

"Are you able to see my soul now?"

"Yes, as it is encompassed by the body."

"What does it look like?"

"It looks much like the earthly body, yet it is of a pure nature. The pureness of nature is the light in which it consists of, for though it looks like the body, it contains no imperfections."

"So a man will look the same in Heaven as he does on earth?"

"'Tis a look much the same; yet the blemishes of human sin be removed, thus changing the appearance in a most reverent way."

"Albert, are you able to see my spirit also?"

"Yes, as it is the life of the soul. It looks much like that of an electric current pulsating with life."

"When are souls created?"

"The Lord creates them anew, as he does the form of the body."

"At what point in time does the soul join the physical body?"

"When the miracle wonder of life is conceived."

"Then souls are created at the moment of conception?"

"Yes, just as there be a sprout within a seed."

"Albert, does a man's earthly, physical body reunite with his soul in Heaven at some point in time?"

"No, for they dissolve to dust just as they came, and only be of a purpose to contain the soul while on earth; for in Heaven, souls float freely, thus needing not a most weighty anchor of a physical body."

"In Heaven, would my hand pass through a soul if I reached out to touch it?"

"Yes, for ye see only the reflection of the soul, for there be no walls to encapsulate it."

"Does a soul have color the way human skin has color?"

"There is no coloring of the souls, yet they are of distinction."

"What accounts for the differences in strength between souls?"

"'Tis by the strength of the Light in which it is made and the pulsating of the life of the Holy Spirit."

"Albert, when Mule was taken to Heaven all those times, what part of her was actually taken?"

"'Twas so simply the essence of the soul."

"Did her spirit go up too?"

"No, for what remained, was."

"So she was not taken up in spirit?"

"No, for 'twas the ascending of the soul."

"Albert do you think the Holy Spirit is underemphasized by today's church?"

"Yes, for 'tis a most precious gift. And thus it is with him that ye find good things, and they be of a greater ease to thus contain within ye heart."

"Should the Holy Spirit be given equal status to God and Jesus?"

"Not necessarily. Yet be there no mistake upon the gift of his value, as he transcends many a soul, just as in the same way as the Father and the Son."

"Does the Holy Spirit have gender?"

"'Tis a Spirit of the Lord, thus 'tis a he."

"Does the Holy Spirit have form or shape?"

"No, for 'tis much like that of a powerful gift of love."

"What did Jesus mean when he said the 'Kingdom of God is within you'?"

"As the gift of the Holy Spirit fills ye heart and ye love be in Jesus, he (Jesus) is in ye. Thus the Kingdom is also."

"Albert, what can you tell me about the spiritual gift called 'speaking in tongues'?"

"One would be most wary, as it could be a deception of the Evil One to thus pass himself off as an event produced by the Lord. Yet in an instance of time, it could be a Divine event in which angels deep in spirit come forth through the voice of another. Yet this is often rare."

"You mean that if speaking in tongues is not a demonic deception and is truly from the Lord, it is angels speaking and not the individuals?"

"Yes, for the spirits of angels may thus reveal themselves, whereas a mortal man be not of such knowledge while in a deep state of prayer."

"Albert, why would Satan counterfeit speaking in tongues?"

"One may pass a dollar bill of insincere paper in order to deceive the keeper of the store to think his register be full, as in a church; yet the teachings of the church may not be of true Christianity. Thus 'tis best to observe the store for its goods before placing all ye trust in the keeper of the store."

"What do the angels say when they speak in tongues?"

"'Tis not a deed of ease to calculate the currents in a sea of mystery; yet at times, 'tis possible to repeat the sounds which were the first to be uttered by the noble Adam."

Conversation 2

Satan

'Tis a mighty tail the slimy fool doth have.

— Albert

"Albert, could a man tolerate the sight of Satan's soul?"
"No, for 'tis a horror far beyond imagination."

"Can you tolerate the sight, Albert?"

" 'Tis a most unpleasant experience, for to see what has fallen be not a sight to behold with glory."

"Does Satan resemble a human being?"

"There be some of great distortion."

"How large is he?"

"He be not large like that of an elephant, but he be larger than a man. The soul has many mounds, for his wickedness turned upon him, magnifying his ugliness."

"Does Satan have a tail?"

" 'Tis a mighty tail the slimy fool doth have."

"Does he have horns?"

"No, for 'tis a whimsical detail dreamed up by that of man, perhaps by a cartoonist. Yet he has many disfigurements resembling that of horns."

"Does he have a forked tongue?"

" 'Tis quite true, for would ye expect otherwise from one who speaks not an ounce of truth? The fine division comes in that of the separation of the tongue, as on momentous occasion he speak of truth only as a snare, thus capturing the prey like a fly to that of a finely woven web."

"Did Satan aid in the creation of any part of the earth?"

"'Twas known in advance that Satan would fall, thus he aided in the molding of those of the volcanoes."

"What was Satan's function before his fall from Heaven?"

"He was the supreme creation; yet as the earthly would say, it thus went to his head. He also believes he was given the gift of evil."

"The gift of evil?"

"Just as Mozart is a composer for the angels, Beethoven for the animals, and Van Gogh wields the colorful palette, Satan believes he has a gift for evil and thus feels compelled to use it."

"He's absolutely crazy, Albert."

"Most maliciously so, for he deceives himself, even while deceiving others."

"Was Satan cast down the moment he thought to rebel?"

"No, for our Lord is very loving. Yet when discipline fails, the results be most stern."

"What discipline did the Lord attempt on Satan?"

"Trying to make a fool see the error of his ways be a most difficult task at best, thus there be many lessons. Yet 'tis best not to speak of what was between the Mighty One and Satan, for it be on his path, just as the Lord deals with each person individually."

"When will everyone confess Jesus as Lord?"

"'Tis at the time when the physical being subsides. Satan did so at the time of his falling, yet he does remain to rebel so."

"Did Hell already exist when Satan was cast down?"

"Yes, for intentions were so of a great emptiness; yet one may have known there was to be a primary tenant most deserving of such a dwelling."

"Did Satan know Jesus was born the Messiah?"

"Satan knows all from the beginning of existence, for he also has omnipotence—only it is of the wrong spirit."

"Since Satan knew Jesus would not sin, why did he tempt him in the desert?"

"The arrogance of his powers to thus test the downfall. A blinded fool never ceases to try his powers."

"Why does Satan continue to fight God when he knows he has already lost?"

"It is said as long as people roam the earth, he shall try to bring them to their downfall, for he feels the mightiness of a king. If but one soul falls, 'tis a victorious ennui."

"If Satan asked God for forgiveness, would he be forgiven?"

"Of that, I know not an answer as solid as the earth, for it be a decision of the Master. Yet I believe it to be so, though Satan be filled with arrogant pride and think not to ask."

"Albert, is Satan responsible for hindering my work on the book?"

"Ye be much like the target of a pest, trying for his downfall out of its most despicable nature. The Evil One likes not knowledge displayed, for 'tis much like that of peering into a mirror and seeing the inner true self in opposition to the primped exterior, which cannot be concealed in truth. Thus also, the wicked like not their evil manipulations revealed for all to know and thus be aware to guard against. Be he not pleased for the forthright emission of the words of knowledge to the ears of the world of earthly reality."

"He provides me with a lot of motivation to continue, Albert."

"Much like motivating a lobster to jump out of a pot."

"What is the significance of 666?"

"'Tis a symbol most associated with Satan; yet as to the value of, or how it came to be, I know not, lest it be the double of the Trinity."

"Perhaps a mocking counterfeit or parody of the Holy Trinity?"

"'Tis most possible."

"Albert, how is Satan different from the majority of demons?"

"He be more of a violent nature."

"Since Christians are commanded to have no hate in their hearts, is it wrong to hate Satan?"

"To love him would be to defy the Lord. In the context of character, 'tis most assuredly correct to despise the scum upon the pond."

Conversation 3

Earthly Trials

There are many different sizes of hurdles, for each has a different length of legs.
— Albert

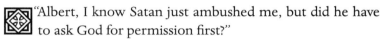"Albert, I know Satan just ambushed me, but did he have to ask God for permission first?"

"Satan asks not for permission, for he knows the limits and also that of which would not be graciously granted; hence he leaps forth from his haunches knowing quite well he may face a battle. 'Tis not a battle in terms of confrontation, for 'tis a battle to apply towards the ending for which the purpose was intended. What he desires may not be the outcome, yet the dust rises and twists around in the air. He asks not for permission, for he acts on his own. Yet the Mighty Hand pounds down at the limit, thus casting a stone to the ground."

"So Satan initiates the trial, but God limits it?"

"'Tis true in some cases; yet observation from the Tower helps predict when the lighthouse must be turned on for the warning of the ships."

"Are you saying that God is responsible for some trials, Albert?"

"Trials be sent for purposes of learning: some be of the Lord and some be of the Evil One, for he tests all."

"Does God himself sometimes send tragedies?"

"At times events may not always be as they appear: for what may seem like a tragedy may be a Gentle Hand touching a soul, thus saving it from a much more horrible fate."

"Does God allow his children to be tested by Satan?"

"'Tis most true, and some obstacles be meant for overcoming—also to identify ye weaknesses and needs, much like a beetle on a leaf. Thus one isolates them and learns well of their uses and outcomes."

"Albert, why were the restraints removed from Satan at this time?"

"At times, though it be not understood, happenings flow smoothly; thus perhaps he becomes in thoughts furthest to the back of the mind. Thus he be allowed to rile up the waters so as ye build a stronger temple."

"It sometimes seems that God allows Satan to get away with too much."

"'Tis best to address the Master, yet I believe it to be for purposes of learning and strengthening. Ye well know there is always a purpose at hand. Also, at times, the deeds of the devil be allowed: for though he think it a victory for the meats for himself, 'tis allowed to be the spoils unto him as the prey escapes into much better boundaries."

"Could Lucinda give me more protection, Albert?"

"She may not always lift you up and carry you over the obstacles on ye path. Be ye known by the weight of the burdens on ye shoulders."

"Why must a man even have trials at all?"

"They be sent as a test of ye faith, yet upon entering the Kingdom, all questions be answered. Then, ye true purpose be most fulfilling. There is much splendor in that of the Kingdom."

"Albert, are the inequities of this life compensated in Heaven?"

"Yea, for when the trial be over, the battle is won, and many rewards await those with faith."

"Why do some men have more trials than others?"

"'Tis much like plants in need of water: for some require much, some minimum."

"Why are some trials greater than others?"

"There are many different sizes of hurdles, for each has a different length of legs."

"It is a difficult concept to fully comprehend, Albert."

"All trials, whether large or small, will be of a purpose most mysterious; for all individuals there be many with a magnitude as varied as the pattern of the snowflake, yet are to be endured."

"Albert, it seems as though sometimes a man is thrown into Satan's clutches for no identifiable reason."

"At times to test the true sturdiness of the driftwood, it must be thrown into violent waters to thus know of its ability to float no matter how turbulent. Many situations be a test of the mighty Evil One which must be faced to let him observe ye buckle not under his forces. Thus it is wise to say that much strength shall be demanded from ye at times. Hence store it up as the stem of a flower stores the water."

"Is there any relationship between a man's stubbornness and the number of trials he must endure?"

"Yes, for there be many lessons to learn. Hence if a mule could carry a full load, there be no reason to go back up the hill; yet if he takes only what he thinks is necessary, thus he creates the extra trip."

"I am going to attempt to summarize my understanding, Albert: The Lord observed that I was not being wise in certain ways; he knew that Satan would take advantage beforehand; Satan did take advantage, but the Lord allowed him to for refining purposes; Satan would have liked to do much more, but the Lord limited him to what would be in my best interests; and at no time was the situation beyond the Lord's control. Is that an accurate summary?"

"'Tis the same engineering as when a lily pad floats upon the water: 'Tis visible it floats when resting on aiding support. For though a frog may happen by and tip the edges neath the water, once he leaves, they float once more upon the surface."

"Is that a yes or a no, my friend?"

"Would you rather I address a simple 'yes'?"

"Yes, at times, Albert, I would rather you address a simple 'yes.' It's easier to understand and *much* easier to punctuate when put to paper."

"'Tis simply the complexity in which we converse, as at times ye understand not the phrasing of my ways, and I may have little comprehension for the intensity of ye wisdom."

"Albert, can you tell when I am joking with you?"

"Rye wheat be of its own distinction."

Conversation 4

Predestination

If it is done, it is God's will.

– Albert

"Albert, why do some friendships fade with time?"

"The intertwining of paths man walks upon are but planned in advance; for crossing into one another is to bring enrichment to life, some even to a joyful destiny when merged until the final day. Be it known that there is a prearranged purpose to fulfill when meeting up with another along the trail of life if ye paths join, even if but for a short while. When the paths sever, 'tis due to that of the purpose having been met, thus one must continue on. For 'tis much like that of crossing a bridge: To hold memories dearly is of value, yet to turn back in search of where the paths once joined is not to go forth as intended. Branching off would not come to be unless 'twas meant to be so."

"Who plans the paths we walk on earth?"

"From start to finish and that of the length in between be preplanned by the Master Architect himself."

"Albert, does God plan even the smallest details of the path?"

" 'Tis true in the majority of ways. Sometimes when a shadow consumes a soul there may be a brief unplanned moment quicker than the wink of an eye, yet 'tis not out of control as one may think while enduring a situation."

"Could I have avoided helping Mule?"

"Yes, yet to follow an evil shadow is ever so sorrowful, for to be pulled from a current of great strength of direction is to follow the Evil One. Yet with the prompting of the soul and the guidance given, one may stray back upon the intended way only to have missed a few pebbles, yet to gain the ultimate end."

"Albert, I know someone who is actively opposed to God and his teachings. Should I seek this person out and try to let him know what is at stake?"

"A sincere deed of the heart be most worthwhile, yet to be guided to the side would be most expected. For indeed, he be in grave condition in those values thus binding the heart."

"Do you mean that God would guide me to the side, Albert?"

"Yes, for at times, things be allowed to happen."

"Why does God create souls destined for Hell?"

"'Tis a complexity much like the strands in the stalk of the plant, as for exact reasons, I know not. Yet it may seem to be so as for the influences those souls would have on others, perhaps to bring about belief in others, or to test the ones of strength."

"Albert, are you saying that man is predestined?"

"One may be happier knowing he has choices to make; yet if things were not meant to be so, they would not happen. This be in the parting of the paths and most all events on life's trails. 'Tis only the foolish man who takes the credit for all his accomplishments and failures."

"Is there any way to know God's plans for a man's future earthly life?"

"No, as the dimensions are most unforeseeable in the implementation of planning."

"Then how does a man know God's will?"

"If it is done, it is God's will."

"Albert, is it futile to make plans for the future?"

"'Tis acceptable to make them for the comfort of one's own mind: for if they are meant to be, they shall come to pass; and if not, one must not question the altered course of events, for they be in ye best interests."

"How do prayers help if everything is predestined?"

"To ask in faith may thus change a trail."

"Albert, that is a complex concept."

"The cresting of arrangements is of a most difficult understanding. 'Tis a mystery most unsolvable."

"Why does it seem to me that I have free will when making choices, Albert?"

"'Tis a topic of great depths, for the thinking and the being of the true reality may appear ever so different: one may think he has a lily in his hand, for 'tis what he perceives—yet his neighbor may say, 'ah, but it is a rose.'"

"But it must be one or the other: a lily or a rose."

"'Tis always that of which the Master creates."

"Albert, is it impossible for the human mind to reconcile the perception of free will with the reality of predestination?"

"'Tis impossible, yet when ye ascend into that of Heaven, ye shall see and wonder how it could be so easy."

"It seems that it takes quite a while to get there, my friend."

"Though there be many a weary traveler, the destination always arrives at the proper point in time."

Conversation 5

Children

For reasons I know not of, the soul of this baby was most needed in Heaven and is of great importance there.

— Albert

"Albert, besides God, is there a specific soul in Heaven who is assigned to watch over the children of the earth?"

"No, as many angels enjoy this chore, for it be of much ease and delight to gaze upon a child of innocence with innocent eyes of wide."

"It must be difficult for angels to watch children who are starving to death."

"'Tis most sorrowful to look upon the children of famine on earth, for 'tis with much sadness to see one have not adequate nourishment to aid in his needs; yet they arrive at the Kingdom."

"Where did the children in Luther's chorus come from?"

"From those whose parents worshipped the opposite, and thus the child adapts to the thinking. And at times it has influences of its own not known by others, thus not calling attention to a need to be set upon a proper path."

"Albert, a married couple who are friends of mine wanted me to ask you a question: Was it God's will for their unborn child to die, and if so, why?"

Albert said: "At times tragedies happen out of love: for though they are greatly saddening in nature, there be a lesson or purpose for those who endure it. For reasons I know not of, the soul of this baby was most needed in Heaven and is of great importance there. Thus ye should not be sad; for 'twas taken to perform works of the Lord, and ye shall be reunited when ye ascend to the Kingdom. And while on earth, ye home shall not be empty, for 'tis most possible to replace what was taken with the same love. So 'tis best not to think of tragic matters as punishments or disciplines, but rather of Divine intention, fulfilling a loving need ye may not understand."

"Albert, did the unborn child ascend to Heaven as it was, or did it ascend as an adult?"

"When ye are called forth, your soul goes upward just as it is when the time arrives."

"Will the child ever become an adult?"

"It will grow over time, but age not like the people on the earth. Thus one may call it maturing, like the grapes."

"It seems so pointless for an unborn child to die, Albert."

Albert said: "One must learn 'tis wise to observe that things created in nature are much like humans born of families: For though they be of different names, 'tis with great ease that they may thus resemble one another in features. Flowers are by far one of the most complex of creations, for one family hath many a brand of offspring. One who would study most closely the complexities could then be in awe of the wonders of nature, for there is much splendor in the study of creation.

"And know that as it is with each flower of the field, it is so with each individual soul: For God loves ye all one by one with ye differences, as he does each flower of the field. For though it resembles a grouping of many, if looked at closely, there would be a difference not to be called a flaw.

"'Tis also much like that of a snowflake: For though observed collectively ye see a glistening field of white crispness, a single flake is of a difference not to be classified as greater than or lesser than, but rather appreciated for the markings which make it beautiful unto itself. And though it may melt after a mere second, for the time it existed, it was a flake of intricate design, specially created for the purpose of being a part of nature."

"Albert, what purpose might their child fulfill in Heaven?"

"Tiny souls of innocent love may be needed to aid other souls of an undeveloped nature which belong in the Kingdom just as rightfully, yet need to share a caring hand; for they may have been destroyed by the hands of man before emerging to the light of life. Though they exist neath the light of the Lord's smile in Heaven, they may need a bond to watch over them. For perhaps that be the appointed purpose of the tiny soul which was taken before its time."

"Could the child be taken from earth to Heaven for an adult's benefit?"

" 'Tis quite true in both ways, as an adult soul may need more development in certain aspects, while also a tiny soul never given the chance of life may be in need of nurturing from one made of love and taken for this purpose."

"Albert, why does God sometimes allow children to be born to abusive parents?"

"There be many reasons too numerous to mention: Yet perhaps 'tis to teach a parent the gift of love who would be of a hard heart minus a child. And at times, it could be so that the child learns of love through his belief in Jesus; for if the child were given love at home, he may never learn of this love for the Lord. Also at times, it may be a strengthening experience, for purposes may not always be known, just as the various hurdles in each individual's life. For though they differ, they are as intense to each one and must be overcome in some manner.

"Yet forget not the influence of Satan in the world: for at times it is of a much greater ease to blame the Lord for not frosting the cake in a fancy way, when it is Satan who makes the cake dry so the frosting cannot adhere."

Conversation 6

Hell

'Tis a crackling core of death-defying screams.

– Albert

"Albert, is Hell located within the earth's core?"

" 'Tis not associated with that of the earth. Just as Heaven is so high above, so is Hell so far below. 'Tis in the rumbling depths beneath the Universe, out of reach of anything known to man."

"Where is the pit?"

"The pit goes far beyond the depths of Hell."

"Albert, what does a person who is going to Hell experience at the moment of death?"

"They would be in total darkness, spiraling downward to the very depths. Yet they go not alone, for they are happily greeted and escorted by the demons."

"What is the most tolerable part of Hell like?"

" 'Tis much like roaming a darkened tunnel with very little air, as for what there is, is heavy with a molding smell of decaying flesh. As one stumbles, he is in despair of feeling trapped, and thus not finding his way cleared to an exit of evil hospitality."

"Are they isolated or with others, Albert?"

" 'Tis of both ways, for one may stumble upon another in the darkness. Yet mostly they be of an austere nature of isolation."

218

"Are there any demons around?"

"They echo sounds of enchanting playfulness."

"What is the worst part of Hell like?"

"'Tis a crackling core of death-defying screams."

"Is it hot, Albert?"

"'Tis of a most searing heat, worse than that of a branding cow; yet they see the guards who gaze upon them most determined not to let them flee, ever taunting them with laughter."

"How is the pit different from the rest of Hell?"

"The space in the pit is sealed with solitude. Each soul which gets cast upon the pit is encapsulated in a torment of solitude blanketing their wicked ways."

"Albert, in what part of Hell is Luther?"

"Those ushered into the pit by the Mighty One's aid thus fall to destruction to their own ways, for they be sealed in the fire."

"Does Satan like it in Hell?"

"'Tis something I know not of, yet one would question why he roams the earth in great frequency."

"Can you tell me anything else, Albert?"

"I know not the intricate workings of the innkeeper, as 'tis not a hotel in which I have visited to stay."

Conversation 7

The End Times

> Millions of moons shall pass. The years be so far in advance, there be no accurate count.
>
> – Albert

"Albert, what is the key to understanding the Book of Revelation?"

"Setting the images into action that are thus written about, for it is to imagine well how great the power of the Lord's return."

"Is it written in primarily figurative or literal language?"

"Figurative, for in reality, one would not see such images: yet they be most stimulating, worthy of reflecting thoughts."

"What is the 'abomination that causes desolation' that Jesus spoke of as a sign of the end of the age?"

"'Tis much like that of a desert in need of water: for though the cactus be contained of water, a passerby reaches not forth; for he fears more from the picks of the thorns, thus keeping him from the juice within."

"Albert, what can you tell me about the one known as the Antichrist?"

"A reality like pure spring waters swiftly flowing, allowing for view of glistening rocks. Yet a boulder of overstatement need not block the flow of the river."

"Will the Antichrist know who he is when he is a child?"

"Yes, as one plants a petunia purposefully, it roots well into the ground given."

"Albert, will the Antichrist be a leader of politics, religion, or the military?"

"One of religion, much like that of an extension of the limb upon the tree, and so real, one who sees the color may wish to touch the fruit to believe its existence and experience its juices."

"So Satan's counterfeit of Christ will be quite a believable one. Right, Albert?"

"'Tis as correct as the home of a bird be its nest."

"Has the Antichrist's religious doctrine begun to take shape?"

"'Tis much like that of a candle which wax becomes softened, and thus it slowly trickles into a new dimension."

"Albert, is the 'man of lawlessness,' spoken of in the Book of Revelation, the same person as the Antichrist?"

"Oh, such depths ye mind be of, yet I could say only that I would believe so. Yet this be of the future, so I know not the absolute, like a seed on the wind glides on the air, yet does not know where he landeth."

"What can you tell me about the battle of Armageddon?"

"I know not the earthly plans; yet in the heavens, the Lord's legions be arrayed twelve across."

"Are the legions comprised of angels, Albert?"

"They be mainly angels, yea, even the formidable Herman and Tyrone on the right flank, with Annihilator, the fastest and most powerful horse of creation in their midst."

"Who are Herman and Tyrone?"

"They be mighty holy warriors among the angels, walking with steps of thunder and playing a most joyful game of Ping-Pong—with Satan being the ball."

"What color is Annihilator?"

"White, most naturally, kind sir—with eyes of blue."

"Why did God name him Annihilator?"

"He tramples the demons till they are no more."

"Albert, who commands each of the twelve legions?"

"'Tis best to address the Master, for the names be held in much secrecy. Yet I say they be appointed men of earth, only three having ascended, the others yet to fulfill their earthly lives."

"Albert, will the Antichrist come in this generation? I know you don't know exactly, but just an approximation please."

"Millions of moons shall pass. The years be so far in advance, there be no accurate count."

"When Jesus returns to earth, will that be the end of human life on earth?"

"Only the Master may say for sure, but 'tis my belief 'tis so."

Conversation 8

The Creation

'Twas a most preposterous little mind to think of the descent of man as swinging from vines.

— Albert

"Albert, did God or Jesus create the Universe?"

"Many things are in unison just like that of a vine: for though they join together and branch out, the fruit doth produce the total wine."

"Is it possible for Creation and Evolution to both be true?"

"Yes, for 'tis much like that of a budding flower: for at first there appears a mere bud, and yet with the passing of eons of time, it slowly unfolds until the smile of each petal is seen as the entirety of the flower."

"Albert, did the Creation take God a literal six days to complete?"

"No, for each day be molded in that of two hundred years. 'Twas a most consistent process, and, oh, what a glorious job he did."

"Are you counting years as we on earth count them now?"

"No, for 'tis figurative in relation to understanding, as I know not the intrinsic value of all these calculations; for 'tis not a concern from the perspective in which I dwell. Thus there are areas in which I have little understanding: for my boundaries be limited in some purposes, just as there are many varieties of flowers seen for different types of adornments or vegetations; and angels of different functions, as many speak not as I am allowed."

"Was the Creation of the earth completed after Satan's rebellion?"

"Yes, for 'twas a loving project."

"Since man is predestined, why does God have man live on earth at all?"

"To experience the blessed miracle of birth and life."

"Albert, is there human life anywhere in existence except here on earth?"

"No, for the earth contains all the Lord was mindful of."

"Why did God create stars?"

"When the angels fell, the stars were created to keep the darkness from the heavens, for the Lord knew well in advance that the evil could live only in darkness: thus he protected the Universe with the stars."

"Albert, were Adam and Eve the first humans on earth?"

"Yes, most definitely."

"What about the belief that man evolved from apes?"

"'Twas a most preposterous little mind to think of the descent of man as swinging from vines."

"Was Adam created before or after the 'day of rest'?"

"Man was created well after the 'day of rest.'"

"Albert, when did the dinosaurs roam?"

"Much before Adam and Eve, before the completion of the earth."

"Did they become extinct before Adam and Eve?"

"Yes, for they were overcome with the existence of other creations."

"How did the different races come into being?"

"A form of adaptation to the lands in which ye survive, thus becoming races unto themselves; just as all origins of people evolved into a culture distinguishing them, much like the markings of the animals of the wild."

"When was North America first inhabited, and by whom?"

"I know not in time frame, only that there was an Indian-like people as a migration from the northern lands."

"Albert, who was Cain's wife?"

" 'Tis not written of Hester."

"Where did Hester come from?"

"Many things be not of script, for they be of many a descent."

"Did all the children Adam fathered come through Eve?"

"She was his appointed mate in good times and bad."

"Albert, does that mean that Adam fathered children through another woman?"

"Ye be of quite the inquisitive nature, hence some mysteries remain to be marveled. If a man were to learn the facts to too many a questions, 'twould spoil the direction and desire to seek God; hence there be many lessons taught in the Kingdom."

Conversation 9

Original Sin in the Garden of Eden

'Tis much like that of a dinner: for not a morsel should be taken without God's blessing first.

— Albert

"Albert, where is the original Garden of Eden?"

"A parched parcel of Sudanese desert where the rivers once ran."

"The rivers moved?"

"Things often change with time, for surely this be a time of long ago."

"Albert, what did the Garden of Eden look like?"

" 'Twas modeled after the Lord's Garden of Knowledge and Contemplation in Heaven."

"Do you mean the one where he spoke to Mule?"

"Yes."

"Albert, when Satan tempted Eve in the Garden of Eden, did he actually appear to her as a serpent?"

"Yes, for 'tis easier to cast attention unto a normal appearance of a creature found amidst a garden floor. Be it also to imply the adage, for the characteristics of Satan be much like a snake: sly, slimy, and most death exhibiting."

"Did he audibly speak to Eve, or did he simply place thoughts in her mind?"

"'Twas most audible."

"Didn't Eve think it was somewhat unusual to hear a snake talking, Albert?"

"When one is captivated in a most trance-like manner, they stop not to question the peculiarities of the situation."

"Which evil spirit specifically tempted Eve?"

"A created spirit of Satan found most tempting to man, thus assuring a downfall to sin."

"Albert, do you mean the Demon of Lust was responsible for man's fall in the Garden of Eden?"

"Ye be of a most austere awareness, thus others see ye as being of an odd species, like an elephant without a trunk."

"So lust is the original sin?"

"'Tis much like that of a dinner: for not a morsel should be taken without God's blessing first."

"What I understand you to say, Albert, is that Adam and Eve had sexual intercourse, but that it would have been permissible if they had asked God first. Is that accurate?"

"Yes, for then it would have been blessed."

"Had it never crossed their minds to have sexual intercourse before this time?"

"That is correct."

"Albert, is it significant that lust was the original sin instead of some other sin?"

"Merely that it is a matter of a most common nature."

"How is sexual intercourse, prompted in this instance by the Demon of Lust, equated with the 'tree of the knowledge of good and evil'?"

"The 'tree of the knowledge of good and evil' be not the deed of sexual intercourse itself, but the decision taken of their own initiative to decide of themselves what was permissible or not, in opposition to God's command."

"What does the 'tree of life' represent?"

"'Tis symbolic of God's plan."

"So, Albert, what is the meaning of Genesis 3:22?"

Albert said, "The man has tried to usurp the authority of God and the Son; but salvation is of God, not man, and thus will eternally remain so."

Conversation 10

Male and Female

The woman would drown in midstream from the briefest glimpse to the side to catch the light reflecting upon her hair.
— Albert

"Albert, in the Book of Genesis, what did God mean when he said to the woman, 'your husband will rule over you'?"

"The stronger ones of character are thus the males; hence it is so they have the sternest of words, for 'tis a gift given them by the Lord—as every porch must have a strong pillar to uphold the roof of the house. 'Tis not a man of sturdy backbone to bow in demands of woman."

"So God gives males dominion over females?"

"'Tis a status assigned from Above; for each has a purpose, none above the other."

"Albert, what do you think of political movements such as feminism?"

"'Tis as unnatural and uncalled for as planting roses in a hayfield, for there be no legitimate purpose."

"In general, how are the women of today different from women of the past?"

"It seems as though their thinking and precepts deteriorate with the advancement of time."

"Would Lucinda agree with that analysis, Albert?"

"She be of a much superior thinking than an earthly woman; and knowing the purpose intended for their performance as female, she is in complete agreement. In the words of Lucinda, 'women should be fenced in and know their boundaries.'"

"Is it acceptable for women to be priests?"

"As long as the Word be spoken of truth from the heart, it matters not—though men are more masterful."

"In what way, Albert?"

"The instincts of the stronger species be much quicker and of a wiser rationality, thus they survive the swim of the river to deliver the oats of proper nutrition. The woman would drown in midstream from the briefest glimpse to the side to catch the light reflecting upon her hair. The Lord sent forth the Son, and be it not of error."

"What do you think when some people suggest that God is a woman?"

"Most disapproving, for 'tis blaspheme, for our Lord is who he says he is. To believe otherwise is to be a mocker."

"Albert, I know a woman whose marriage plans just fell through. She is driving herself crazy about it—and me too."

"There is a most important lesson to acknowledge in nature: For the bee is joined with the flower not only by its beauty, but also for its purpose. Yet if the flower reaches forth for the glistening fingers of the sun before its time, it may miss the bee; for it will have drained itself of the succulent juices from its roots, thus causing it to wither. Hence, 'tis best to be like that of a flower: For though some start from bulbs, it may seem ever so slow to peek through the soils and rise out. Yet behold: for one day it will be in bloom of fullness smiling to all, thus beckoning the bees, and hence, life's renewal."

Albert added, "Her guardian angel, Caroline, will also speak of this."

Caroline said: "She is woefully weak at the boundaries; weak at heart; lapsing in faith. Out of the depths of desperation of her own mind, she bypasses the peace of the Lord. She causes her own problems. This leaves the window open for self-doubt to fly in like the raven of death.

"She is allowed to make herself heartsick in hopes of learning from her despair. That is why it is allowed to happen: not as a punishment, but as a lesson. It falls on deaf ears, as she listens only to her heart's desire.

"Seek not self-worth in men or others, for this is a gift of the Lord which should not be overlooked. Other people have no command of it. Freedom comes more easily when we do not resist the lessons of the Lord. Learn these now, for how can one love freely when feasting on childlike fantasies and not on reality? There is no perfect man riding on a white horse."

"Albert, is divorce ever permissible?"

"When two plants join at the roots, they thus enter that of a binding relationship till the days dwindle down and one is called forth. Thus if a storm shakes one plant violently and the other sways not, the strength of one shall feed the other. 'Tis best to seek aid when the binding roots become disrupted by evil soil, for to abandon a troubled one would only but leave it in isolation as an offering to the soils of darkness. With the Lord as the guiding gardener, the plants shall grow in unison as thus intended."

Conversation 11

Demons

'Tis most openly an evil shadow: for the minds of men be not built in such a way as to house a sewer in a garden.
— Albert

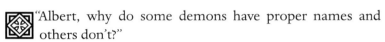"Albert, why do some demons have proper names and others don't?"

"All of God's creation have been given names, but 'tis best to remember some have fallen."

"Since God gave names to all he created, who created generic-name and no-name demons?"

"'Tis best to address the Master, yet I say there be birth of spirit."

"It must be Satan who creates them, Albert. Who else could it be? Why doesn't Satan name the spirit he creates?"

"It takes care to affix a name to a child: hence if he cares not, he would name not."

"So all fallen angels are demons, but not all demons are fallen angels?"

"'Tis most correct in logic."

"What was Luther's function in Heaven, Albert?"

"The dreaded Luther was once an angel of love with many a caring, gentle quality. Yet for those who have fallen, the opposite be true of their deeds."

"You mean *exactly opposite*?"

" 'Tis so."

"Albert, Jesus sealed Luther in the pit, but he lets other fallen angels roam freely. Why?"

"The fallen ones of evil intent who thus ruined the earth seeking destruction of good souls and believe not in the difference of a mightier power of goodness can thus be put to destruction. Their destruction be not necessarily total annihilation, yet they be removed and placed deeply where they can harm no more. For to take up war among many good souls repeatedly be not favored in the eyes of the Lord."

"How do fallen angels feel about lost souls?"

"It brings pleasure like that of being a grand victor; for they are fallen souls which did not accept the truth of life, nor the Master's promises."

"How do the holy angels feel about the fallen angels?"

"In the beginning, we were all of great likeness, then came the House of Great Separation. True purity remains with God."

"Did the fallen angels only make one mistake, and then they were cast down?"

"Yea, for one is all it takes. In the human world, there may be successive tries, for ye be blessed with forgiveness of repentance. Yet when the angels revolted, there was none."

"Albert, did most of the fallen angels freely rebel against God, or were they tricked?"

" 'Twas a ruthless ploy of deception, for none of a knowing mind would choose other than God. 'Tis easy to fall to the power of lies when it be of ye peers, and thus ye think it acceptable without having it cross ye knowledge to inquire of the true Master."

"Why don't more fallen angels rebel against Satan like Simon did?"

"Only the fallen ones thus knowing the difference and wise enough to well understand the ways of their error try forth to rebel, yet 'tis with great struggle. 'Tis possible to be lifted up, yet seldom."

"Do evil spirits ever have access to Heaven—like when Luther showed Mule a vision of Heaven?"

"Only from a distance, yet they distort perception; for what appears near is really quite far away. Be it known that they cannot enter the House of Truth, for they would perish."

"Albert, how can a man differentiate mere human anger versus anger caused by the demons?"

"'Tis much like that of the temperature of burning fire: For a small fire of natural causes emits that of enough heat for survival and the cooking of food; yet a roaring blaze may be most destructive, for it may engulf a building in but a second. So it is with the more extreme the heat, the more destructive the fire."

"So it is mainly a question of degree?"

"Deeds evil in nature be prompted by influences of darkness: the more extreme the input, the more horrible the deed. Yet trivial deeds harmless in nature leading to no set destruction be of man's own doing. Horrid events may be obvious if tracked by the scent; yet man be caught up in judging the inner workings of the human mind, thus the value in seeking the Lord has diminished. If this were not so, there would be far less cruelty in the world."

"Albert, if a believer discerned a demon and ordered it to go, could it remain?"

"If one may sneak into that of a vacant house without being noticed, it may remain; yet if ordered to go by a representative of the Law, he must gather up his belongings and go on to other adventures."

"Would Luther have been more difficult to physically control and evict if he had possessed a strong male instead of Mule?"

"No, for Luther's strength be his own regardless of the capsule. The strength be contained within the spirit."

"But if I didn't isolate the evil spirit from the strong male's spirit, then I would be contending against the strength of both?"

"'Tis quite true, for it casts a shadow of deception."

"Albert, what is a ghost?"

"They speak of spooks, yet there is no such thing as that of a ghost: For those souls gone on to Heaven thus remain so, and those gone down to the depths of the fire be not able to return. Thus a ghost could only be that of an impersonating demon."

"Should believers fear demons?"

"Those standing firm in the soils of the Lord have no fear of wavering from evil winds. Yet to know they exist is of importance, as all be like a birdhouse in the coldest days of winter."

"Albert, can any believer cast out any demon?"

"In a manner of speaking—yet be it known it takes one of great strength to achieve the difficult."

"Demons leave more quickly when I am aggressive with them. Why?"

"Legs be no mightier than sticks, only lest ye give them more authority. But behold: no matter what the size, they all become fragile as toothpicks when confronted."

"Can a man command a demon to go away by just thinking the command?"

"'Tis best to be harsh like that of a bear attacking its prey, for then there be no mistake as to who is master."

"Albert, why do some demons leave immediately when commanded to do so and others delay?"

"It be due to that of pure foolishness: for they shall evidently have to flee when on grounds of purity where they shall not survive."

"What if a mocker commanded a demon to depart?"

"They shall remain, for 'tis much like that of a child in a garden: as he would not step to the side if requested by a stranger; yet if he saw a snake thus posing a threat, he would run to the safety of the riverbank."

"Would a mocker be in danger by giving such a command?"

"Yes, for one of the same element may fight against another, for they have not the protection of the Holy Hand."

"Albert, what percentage of people in the world can be possessed by a demon, even if but for a short while?"

"Most sorrowfully, one-third *(8% in the U.S.).* There be a lower percentage where the Word is preached, higher where 'tis not. In the mire of the bog, the Wicked Finger touches many."

"How many of these people are severely possessed?"

"Half again the number mentioned *(16% worldwide, 4% in the U.S.).*"

"Albert, out of the multitudes of those with demon problems, how do I know which ones to focus my attention on?"

"A puppy crying, with its foot caught in the fence, help it loose; a rock in a hole, let it go."

"How often does Satan himself possess a soul?"

"'Tis a very rare occasion: for there be many to dispatch with deeds, just as the angels are dispatched from the Lord."

"Is it possible for a demon to possess me?"

"There be no possible opportunity under Heaven, as such a great light within reveals a prowler in an instant; thus they are forced back into the darkness by the pureness of the light. Hence, only thoughts occasionally pass."

"Albert, was Adolf Hitler demon possessed?"

"There be multitudes of hateful creatures homing in the ruins of a temple: for what was he but a shell of man." [AUTHOR'S NOTE: *Hitler's chief demons were named Lucius and Marcus, who specialized in lies, torment, and projection of blame. Sometime in the early 1990's, I found out they were still alive and wreaking havoc. I asked God how that was possible. God said that although Hitler had been brought before him for judgment by millions of supplicants, no one had ever specifically brought Lucius and Marcus before him. I asked God if he would now judge them. God's verdict was guilty with a sentence of annihilation (a relatively rare sentence for fallen angels).*

Lucius and Marcus are no more. Hitler's soul is in the crackling core of Hell.]

"Is an idle mind the devil's workshop?"

"At times an empty mind is much needed for rest; but that should only be for a short while, as a mind with thought is less likely to be penetrated by idle influences from the evil ones. 'Tis much like that of an empty house: for if the owner returns not on schedule, the vagrants may rob him of the smallest of goods."

"Albert, are there many demon-possessed individuals who reside in prisons and mental health institutions?"

"There be many misunderstood by man. Yet be it known: demons infest all earthly realms, not just ones of high suspicion. Caution be advised."

"Are drug abuse and alcoholism caused by demons?"

"To desire the excesses with a passion most harmful is of the Evil One: for 'tis much like thirsting after polluted waters, to thus not only kill the lake, but all things of value contained within it."

"Albert, could a believer cast a demon out of an alcoholic?"

"Only when they be of controlling progress, much like that of a dog lapping water in the heat of a summer day."

"Are those exhibiting 'multiple personalities' possessed?"

"At times 'tis much like storing furniture in an attic collecting dust, thus only becoming accessible through climbing the stairs; and yet at times it could be a combination of tenacious tentacles of the Evil One."

"Is schizophrenia caused by demons?"

"'Tis most openly an evil shadow: for the minds of men be not built in such a way as to house a sewer in a garden."

"So, Albert, most schizophrenics would have a possessing demon to confront?"

"As likely as the bird finds its nest."

"Then schizophrenia can be eliminated?"

"One may not find it of great ease to cast a daisy into a pea. Be it the world's properties consuming the expectations of behavior-related raindrops: as 'tis most unlikely to see the sun, for the thunder is of great loudness."

"But a schizophrenic could be freed from bondage if they were helped by someone who believed in the Lord and had knowledge of demons?"

"Many a long hour would thus behold a budding crop."

"So the more severe a mental or emotional disorder is, the more likely it is that demons are involved?"

"Yes, for 'tis much like the sweet grass found most nourishing to the horse: for the Lord would not mow the mangled mind lest there be an intent of his own for the benefit of others in the learning of lessons."

"Albert, will the knowledge contained in these writings set the field of psychology straight?"

"One may hack away at the strongest weed, yet it be most difficult to clear the entire field."

"It is tedious work."

"Ye be much like that of the finest racehorse expected to pull a plow."

Conversation 12

Illness and Healing

To ask in faith is a most noble deed, yet the Lord will only heal where intended.

— Albert

"Albert, are human organ transplants acceptable to God?"

"Yes, for sharing the gift of life be a most blessed offering."

"Are test-tube babies acceptable?"

"'Tis not a wise thing to mix science with nature, for the Lord has ways of providing."

"Albert, was Jesus ever physically ill on earth?"

"No, yet he knows well of discomforts and sickness; for he cares so for his children, the healings show compassion and love."

"Who causes physical illnesses on earth?"

"There be those things common to all such as a cold, yet some grave illnesses be brought about by the wicked."

"Why would God allow the wicked to cause a grave illness like cancer in one of God's own children?"

"Perhaps to wake up those with a hard heart, fast asleep."

"But, Albert, many softhearted people are afflicted with cancer."

"Only if it be the Lord's will, just as those who are healed."

"But only the wicked cause it?"

"Yes, and at times it be their downfall: for to cast a soul in that of critical condition oftentimes sharpens their senses, thus they turn and knoweth the true need of the Lord."

"So God will not heal all his children of all diseases and illness simply because they ask in faith?"

"To ask in faith is a most noble deed, yet the Lord will only heal where intended."

"Will God himself sometimes make an individual sick?"

"Only in the way of loving discipline: for in times of trouble, one's mind thinks more intensely; thus 'tis best to slow some down."

Conversation 13

The Seats of Power

They revolted like peasants against the Great King, thus being seen as favorable in the eyes of Satan.

— Albert

"Albert, why did the forces of evil plant that vision in Mule's mind about Luther coming back to take revenge on her?"

"'Twas a ploy to deceive her into thinking she had been wronged by the disappearance, and thus that he exists still. For 'tis well known the terror she felt of him. A hunter who well knows his prey knows the best snare to set. Yet 'twas only a vision, for Luther be well sealed for eternity."

"Was Satan the hunter who set the snare, Albert?"

"The one who sits at the left hand of Satan."

"Who is that?"

"Zekkube, the warrior-scout, who roams ahead."

"Was Zekkube formerly a holy angel?"

"Yes, he was a mighty angel looking for exotic seeds to transcend to that of the earth upon his orders to supply beauty."

"Albert, who sits at Satan's right hand?"

"The fallen one known as Mazurka: for he takes in his net the ones snared by the Evil Master and discards them unto the places where they fit."

"What was Mazurka's purpose before he fell?"

"Thus as it was in the heavens, he was dispatched to the earth to watch over the animals of the wilds, protecting them from merciless killings."

"Were Mazurka and Zekkube of the same angelic rank as Michael?"

"No, they were of a lesser order, revolting and falling for requesting power not fairly due them."

"For requesting power, Albert, or trying to take power?"

"They revolted like peasants against the Great King, thus being seen as favorable in the eyes of Satan."

"I know Jesus sits at the right hand of God, but who sits at God's left hand?"

"Abraham."

"What is Abraham's function?"

"He ministers to many a chosen one on earth in need of special care, for they be on the border of losing their faith."

"Albert, who else lives in God's Throne Room?"

"The Father, Son, and Abraham be of primary domain, yet perhaps at times the prophets from of old shall tarry there."

Conversation 14

The Word of God

It matters not what one may call the fruits or vegetables, but only that they contain true nutrients.

– Albert

Albert spoke: "Be there many ways to create a pot of beans, hence most shall taste delightful. Yet 'tis wise to test that of each ingredient for purity of truth, for those pots conjured up by the misled may appear most sumptuous. Beware: for if they be tainted with even but a hint of misinterpretation, they shall spoil; while the pot with truthful morsels shall be everlasting."

"Albert, is the Bible truly the Word of God throughout?"

"I know ye ask for others so I say unto them: Be thee not fooled, for 'tis true. What is written is of truth, just as written in blood."

"Are parts of the Bible written in figurative language?"

"As it is with most writings, 'tis not always the actual words that matter, but more to sense the effects of the times."

"Are the words of Jesus literal?"

"The words of the Master were thus written just as spoken. Yet the wise man knows he often spoke in that of parables."

"Albert, what would you say to those individuals who would always insist on literal interpretations of the Bible? For example,

244 FARMER'S CONVERSATIONS WITH ALBERT

what would you say to those who would insist that the earth was created in a literal six days because that is just exactly what the Bible says?"

"To thus speculate is to miss the points of the primary nature in which the statement is to be understood. 'Tis much like that of analyzing a color: for to see the components is to pass the true hue."

"So it is quite possible to read too much into certain passages and lose the simple meaning behind it?"

"'Tis much like a tree of many colors: for though the eye sees much, 'tis still a tree."

"So why do some people dissect the Bible?"

"'Tis much like the separation of a plant to seek the miraculous ways of the inner workings. There shall always be those looking for magical answers, thus missing the facts of the truth. Those who look too far may miss out on the scent of the rose neath their nose."

"Albert, what do you think of all the doctrinal arguments between the truly Christian denominations?"

"'Tis best to pay less attention to the writings upon the seed packages: for when all true flowers of the Lord sprout and blossom, they are of equal beauty, as it matters not from where they be purchased."

"Did Solomon write the Book of Ecclesiastes?"

"Yes, with the help of the Lord and many angels, thus providing visions with which to be told. In Solomon's despair, he was thus uplifted."

"Are the Dead Sea Scrolls authentic?"

"Yes, yet most mysteriously so. The works of the writings be most genuine, though little known."

"Albert, what should my reply be to those critics who will say that these writings contradict the Bible?"

"It matters not what one may call the fruits or vegetables, but only that they contain true nutrients. For the wise man will take the nourishment, praise the Lord, and grow; while the foolish man starves on fruitless debate."

"Should I attempt to clear up the misconceptions that will undoubtedly occur?"

"As a window needs that of occasional cleaning, 'tis wise to do so. Yet if it faces a blank alleyway with trash, let it go. For why would one need to sit and stare out the window only to contemplate that of the trash?"

Conversation 15

Tithes and Offerings

'Tis a principle well rewarded if done in faith, yet 'tis not a necessity.

– Albert

"Albert, does God require that an individual tithe or give a monetary offering to the church?"

"Be it not written anywhere in the Word that 'tis demanded; yet if given unselfishly for the purpose of maintaining a temple, 'tis a kind gesture. Yet be it known 'tis most disgraceful to think one must tithe to hear the Word of the Lord."

"What about where Malachi speaks of 'robbing God'?"

"'Twas a saying of old to tell of discipline, yet it be not a demand. For to turn your heart and love to the Lord be worth so much more than any coin or crop."

"If one chooses to tithe, will God return that tithe with an increase?"

"'Tis a principle well rewarded if done in faith, yet 'tis not a necessity."

"If one does give a tithe or offering, does it have to be given to an organized church?"

"Offerings given in sincerity and of a loving spirit, whether to a specific garden or scattered to the winds of the needy, be appropriate, and thus need no publicity or approval; for it is known what has been done."

Conversation 16

Salvation

When ye forget the Master and to rely on him for help, comfort, and love, all is dangerous.

– Albert

"Albert, how can a man be certain that he has eternal life?"
"To have belief in faith is the most valuable key for entrance to the Kingdom."

"Why does God place so much value on faith?"

"Those who believe without demanding proof of seeing demonstrate a most devout love."

"Is entrance to Heaven by faith alone, or by faith and repentance from sin?"

"Faith is much like the great foundation; yet to repent is to indulge in the acceptance that ye be a mere man, and thus ye acknowledge the glory of the Lord's power in love of forgiveness, as he extends his arms with joy and nay to the ways of reprimand."

"Can a man enter Heaven without a water baptism?"

"Yes, for 'tis by belief in Jesus the Son and God the Lord in which allows entrance to the Kingdom. For water is a celebration and most ceremonial of men as a commitment."

"Should Christians go out of their way to do good works?"

"No, for ye are saved by faith in Christ. It matters not what sacrifices ye make at the altar but what is contained in ye heart that is important. Gifts in the Kingdom be based on the contents of ye heart."

"Albert, what happens to the truly good people who do not believe in Jesus?"

"The Holy Spirit lives in everyone, and if they lead their life on a peaceful path of good knowing and believe in their heart of something better, they shall find Jesus."

"How were people saved before Jesus died for our sins?"

"Led and taught in the belief of God the Father, as there were many before Jesus who spoke true words for many to hear."

"How are the people saved who never hear of God during their earthly lifetime?"

"Of that I know not, for there be many an exception, just as some plants grow well neath the darkness of the trees."

"Albert, once a man has been saved, can he lose his salvation?"

"Yes, for 'tis much like rowing a boat ashore on the sands of safety: If ye be forgetful and revolting and take to the waters without that of an anchor, 'tis most distressful. Yet if ye call on the hands of the Lord to guide the boat ashore, he shall cast you in once again."

"I thought all believers were saved."

"'Tis quite true that if ye believe, ye go to the Kingdom; yet when you deny and renounce Jesus to go on a path of greater ease, many a troubling thing can happen."

"Albert, what is the biggest error a man can make in searching for God?"

"To meditate inward for the answers of ye soul is much like that of tying a millstone around ye own neck, for 'tis of the most opposite direction."

"There are those who teach this way, Albert."

"Misconceived notions, believed and professed, behold much bleakness: as one may never see the light of glory from the shadows of darkness."

"What happens to those who believe that man is his own god?"

"To be absorbed tremendously in one's own thoughts, identifying them as his own and dependent upon himself, not looking upward for inspiration, is to be absorbed in oblivion and thus linger in the depths. Those in search of perfection among themselves be looking in the wrong direction. 'Tis a lesson they must learn in time."

"What if a man truly believes he worships God, but actually worships something more esoteric?"

"To worship a most mystical nature is to thus dwell in the dark shadows. Be it much like that of art in the abstract, thus reality be not at hand; for the spirit must reflect the reality of God the Lord. Woe be to those in the practice of wizardry, for they shall thus form a cloud of their own doing that will hinder their way of truth to the mighty Kingdom."

"Albert, what earthly doctrines are influenced by Satan?"

"Anything oppressing people from the way intended is not a true wish of the Lord. This be so in churches, countries, and most any area that thus stunts a tree from potential development."

"What should children do if their parents teach false doctrine?"

"All yearlings eventually stand firm thus leaving the nursing mother, as nature intends for this to be so; hence it is so also of man. When the milk she bears is of a bad quality, 'tis best to seek nourishment on ye own for what is good than to become of grave nature with an ending of darkness if ye drink of the bad out of guilt or habit."

"What happens to those who die while they are addicted to drugs?"

"Those caught up in the problems of the world, who thus fall to influences of self-betterment in terms of chemical relief for the physical and seek not the miracle of the spiritual, linger on the surface of the darkest shadows."

"Life can certainly be dangerous, Albert."

"When ye forget the Master and to rely on him for help, comfort, and love, all is dangerous."

"Albert, are some sins worse than others?"

"At times, yes, for 'tis reflective of the situation; yet it matters not to what degree, as all are forgiven in a most powerful way."

"If a man commits a crime under Satan's influence, does God hold the man responsible?"

"He be not responsible in the eyes of the Lord; for he knows the heart so well, he could thus call the prompter of the deed by name. Yet the soul should seek forgiveness, knowing well the wrong, and as an offering."

"Albert, is there an unforgivable sin?"

"To reject belief and love in the Lord."

"Other than rejecting God, what sin do you believe puts a man's soul in the most jeopardy?"

"Hatred caught in the heart that is not thus set free by prayer of the Lord can blind a man's eyes and thus cover the realms of reason: for the beauty of love when it is eaten away by hate destroys the goodness of the apple core, and thus it rots away."

"Does God judge ascended human souls by reviewing their earthly sins with them?"

"No, for once ascended, they be welcomed most lovingly, but may be under judgment while on the earth: as 'tis a time in which they may change to turn from evil to good, or repent and seek."

"So there is no judgment once a soul arrives in Heaven?"

"There be little to criticize on a journey of new beginnings."

"Albert, if someone is excommunicated from a church, does this mean they are severed from God?"

"No, for 'tis the politics of mere men, as the Lord well knows the circumstances in full and would thus never abandon a true seeker out of love. And if asked, he forgives."

"Albert, are all homosexuals consigned to Hell when they die?"

"Though they be driven by a lifestyle influenced by the Evil One, if they grow toward a sincere belief of the Savior, his great love shall overcome them, thus allowing entry to the Kingdom. 'Tis wise to remember the love in one's heart is of more true value than outward displays: thus a loving soul with faith is like a nut within the shell; for once the cover is broken, all is known by the true flavor of the meats."

"When those who follow Judaism die, do they go to Hell because they do not believe in Jesus as being the Messiah?"

"They go not to Hell, for they believe in Moses as the Chosen One and God the Father; thus their beliefs be in the proper direction like a daisy reaching forth for the sun, though it goes to seed."

"What about the Bible verse that says Jesus is the only way to the Father?"

"These are the golden seeds of truth for people of faith following Christianity. Yet to go to seed is to mean the passing by while on the earth from seeing the goodness of the Son and the belief in the Son, Jesus, to make the walk of life hand in hand so beautiful and fulfilling while in the gloom of worldly ways; thus they miss the greatest truth in importance while being too busy looking for the sun (Son) over the horizon when it has already been in the sky in full bloom for many a year. 'Tis most sorrowful. Yet to follow Moses and to believe in the Lord our God is to not be submerged in a total gutter of worthless values or untrue religion, as in following vibrations or such other so-called gods. Thus they worship not false gods, but a man that was real and walked the earth in the Spirit of God the Lord."

"Albert, you know there is a misconception among many concerning Jesus' words on this matter?"

"Yes, but it be that of a misconception; for the minds of men interpret such in ways of their own meaning."

"Do most people who commit suicide go to Hell?"

"Yes, if they know not the Lord to turn to him in times of need; yet there are exceptions. It is a deed that puts a great smile on Satan, thus making him feel victorious."

"Does Hell continue for eternity for those who go there?"

"Yes, for it is an ending thus sealed."

"How can one possibly endure all that torment, Albert?"

"'Tis the immortal soul, not to be confused with the body. Remember: the soul may gradually wither, yet never perish."

"Do the people in Hell ever understand what they did wrong?"

"Over time, the misinformation may reveal itself through the ugliness of the fires; yet the results are something I know not of, only that it is possible on the rare occasion to be freed towards the light."

"So, Albert, people are sometimes lifted up from Hell?"

"In an instance, 'tis possible; for lessons may be learned and budding desires of the heart may be blossomed, thus learning the wrong and yearning for what is right."

"But it is rare to be taken from Hell to Heaven?"

"Much like the extinct flowers which once filled the plains. Yet the Master may have exceptions for reasons known only to him."

"Albert, are there more good or evil souls on earth?"

"There be multitudes more of tender souls than wicked: for the proportion of believers and those with light values in their hearts and loving actions far outnumber the wicked schemers and evildoers belonging to Satan, as good far outweighs the carrots of evil."

"What percentage of people who live on the earth go to Hell?"

"Most sorrowfully, one-third *(8% in the U.S.)*. 'Tis frightful to be a mocker."

"Can you break down that percentage by religious groups?"

"No, for 'tis not a question of precision: In Heaven, there be only believers of truth; in Hell, there be only mockers of truth. There be no other demarcations. God draws the line."

Conversation 17

Death

Did not the Lord experience this in the final days knowing well in his heart where he would go?
— Albert

"Albert, when a man dies, is there any delay in going to Heaven?"

"No, for when the Lord calls, ye shall be duly escorted."

"Are so-called 'mercy killings' ever permissible?"

"'Tis not a decision of ye own; for when the Lord comes to claim ye soul, it is well in his hands. And to refuse aid is much like taking ye own life."

"So it is wrong, Albert?"

"One would see the whole as yes, even though to look at each petal of the flower, there be ever so distinct characteristics of each. Yet to pick it away as one is not of honor to the whole."

"So in the rarest of instances it might be permissible?"

"'Tis of mellow correctness, for there is a fine precision."

"Albert, should loved ones ever be withdrawn from life-support machines if withdrawal would mean certain death?"

"'Tis that of a most trying decision, much like that of one sickly rose bush in a beautiful garden of many: For to place a stake in many directions of which to tether the limbs for upward growth is of little use when the root system is paralyzed, not able to take nutrients from the soils and water from the ground. After a point in time in which ye see no response to the tender care given, perhaps 'tis best to lay it to rest and let it become of the soil once more; for the space left may be lonely, yet the love may place a new bush which may go and plenish. Not all things of nature may be prolonged; thus 'tis best to set them free, just as a lame bear returns to its den to die, for 'tis his proper nature to do so. 'Tis also best to set a bird free from a cage than to listen to it cry for its mate, just as a soul cries to go home once more."

"Albert, if these people are meant to die, then why doesn't God just take them when they are attached to the machines?"

"'Tis a question as mysterious as the workings of time: For perhaps the soul is growing or being prepared for the journey to the Kingdom. And in some instances, perhaps what would appear so as a lingering lily brings a lesson or points a purpose to the beloved around, as 'tis not always the submerged soul which suffers: for it may be cared for with a Tender Hand of which the onlookers may not see, yet they have a lesson of strength and faith to learn, as there is a purpose to heartfelt suffering; for 'tis not a punishment as some eyes see it."

"Does God condone capital punishment as administered by men on earth?"

"'Tis that of a distasteful event thought up by man: for the Lord knows discipline, yet he forgives those who ask in sincerity."

"Albert, how does God determine the specific manner of death for one of his children?"

"'Tis reflective of the lesson which must be learned."

"Why does someone need to learn a lesson at death?"

"It impinges upon what one has experienced in life, as one never knowing turbulent times may thus know anguish at the end."

"Do people *really* need to learn anguish, Albert?"

"Yes, for 'tis a lesson of great importance. Did not the Lord experience this in the final days knowing well in his heart where he would go? When one experiences that of true despair, he thus appreciates the glory of the Kingdom more appropriately, for it be the extreme in sweetness."

"What might someone learn by dying of a heart attack?"

"Each individual, being of his own soul, thus may have a lesson different than the other; yet at times it may be so to slow one down and thus reflect his thinking in the way intended, like calm waters."

"What might the lesson be for someone dying quietly in their sleep?"

"Depending upon the soul, it be much like that of a reward for a life well lived, thus succumbing peacefully."

"Do believers have anything to fear from the process of dying?"

"No, for 'tis a rotting of the flesh and not the soul; for their souls must be released to the Homeland."

"Albert, when it is time to die, who actually kills the body?"

"'Tis the mighty touch of the Master."

"Does Satan kill those who will go to Hell?"

"He ensnares the souls who he claims for himself who have thus not seen the light."

"So it is either Jesus or Satan who kill the body?"

"'Tis the commanding touch."

"Albert, I suppose that Satan is not allowed to kill any of Jesus' children. Does Jesus ever kill any of Satan's?"

"'Tis true to the extent of which Satan may not have one belonging to the Lord; but the power of the Lord's hand is mightier, and through his judgment, he may choose."

Conversation 18

Animals

God rejoices in the acceptance of animals of love.
— Albert

"Albert, is it wrong to use animals for medical experiments?"
"Creatures of nature belong as such, for they be of just as much value of greatness as the human animal. 'Tis a cruelness of man, though there be a benefit in the aid of helping humans. In my eyes, 'tis a most grave and unacceptable practice."

"Are animal souls as valuable as human souls in the eyes of God?"

"They are not as man, but they are of great importance."

"Does God punish human souls for abusing animals?"

"Most assuredly, for the animal be defenseless."

"What if a human were cruel to animals, but very good to other humans? Would the human be sent to Heaven or Hell?"

"That decision be of the Father for review of the individual blossoms in the bouquet."

"Is God pleased with humans who share their homes with animals, especially lost and abandoned animals?"

"Yes, for to share ye home with innocent ones of love be a most blessed blossom in ye garden, sprouting a bloom of love and devotion so true, beatified by the smile of the sun (Son?)."

"Albert, do all animals go to Heaven when they die?"

ANIMALS 257

"Only those animals strongest in spirit: for they be mammals; birds, for they be the aviary of song; also others that be strongest of spirit for their grouping."

"Do some animal spirits go to Hell?"

"Nay, for all who go from the earth go to Heaven. God rejoices in the acceptance of animals of love."

"Do animals that ascend to Heaven have guardian angels while on earth?"

"Animals have guardian angels, for they be creatures of God."

"Does my dog, Bentley, have a guardian angel?"

"Jesus calls him 'mastiff mushpot,' for he be of the sweetest nature. How could the lapping of love not have a guardian? Trudy attends him."

"Are there angels who help lost and homeless animals?"

"Yes, for there be many who enjoy this chore. Gelderman helped guide Canopy the cat to ye."

"What angels keep watch over horses?"

"There be many. Be it known that Garibaldi has great knowledge of the running hooves."

"Are animals aware that God exists?"

"Yes, as those gentle-nature thoughts be close at times to the true reality of the Spirit."

"Albert, is it a sin to eat meat?"

"It is a matter of survival; it is therefore provided. It is not seen as sacrificial and harmful; it is seen as sustenance."

"Albert, what do you think about the cruelty of nature, like when a lion viciously subdues his prey?"

"'Tis a way of thinning out the herd, thus making the herd stronger, while the animal which catches its prey becomes stronger through the meat. 'Tis the way of nature."

"Albert, the prey is probably not feeling that philosophical about it at the time."

"'Tis not that of a purposeful torment."

Conversation 19

Chariot and Cherubim

Chariot was the name of a being such as I, yet he fell from the sky in a most sorrowful way.
— Albert

 Albert said, "A chariot is not a cart with wheels."
"What do you mean, Albert?"
"'Tis a cherubim."
"I'm not sure what a cherubim is."
"'Tis much like a chariot, for names of things oft be named for people."
"I'm not sure what you are trying to tell me, Albert."
"Chariot was the name of a being such as I, yet he fell from the sky in a most sorrowful way."
"Are you one of these cherubim too, Albert?"
"'Tis so."
"And you are saying that you and other cherubim are named after this fallen angel named Chariot?"
"'Tis quite true; for we be lesser spirits than he, yet we be."
"So Chariot is a fallen angel now?"
"Yes, he was a mighty warrior among the angels, yet he fell; for he had hoped to fight Satan for lost souls, and thus kept not in mind that God retrieves them."
"So Chariot became a third party, in addition to God and Satan, battling for lost souls?"

"Yes, for he was a warrior of peace and thus was caught in the deceptive snare of limitless boundaries. Woe be to the spirit who goes not where commanded."

"Didn't God warn Chariot to stop disobeying?"

"Be not mistaken, for there were many an occasion on which he was warned; yet he be blinded, and as always, Satan saw a door to secretly open. Thus 'tis best not to go astray of ye commanded territory."

"Albert, is Chariot now subject to Satan?"

" 'Tis most sorrowful to become subservient to the Kingdom of Darkness, for one must surrender to the ways of another's land. It brings me much sadness; yet there be a great lesson, thus I tell ye."

"What does Chariot do now?"

"Satan robbed him of his powers and thus sealed him in the fires. If he were to turn his heart around, he could thus be freed to command the forces of evil."

"Albert, has Chariot ever asked for forgiveness?"

"No, for his arrogance confuses his wrong."

"Are you and the other cherubim like Chariot was before he fell?"

"We are lesser creations in being that we have been given all of his fine traits, less a will of such strongness."

Conversation 20

Heaven

Souls in the Kingdom happily rejoice and are not of earthly concerns as one might suspect: hence there be no desire to look down anymore.

— Albert

"Albert, how many dimensions does Heaven have?"
"Quite simply, uncountable."

"How can humans grasp that?"

"They rely too much on logical senses; and I say to ye, not all things be that way in the Kingdom. For the human mind has not the capacity for understanding the ways of the Mighty One, for the differences between Heaven and earth be of such vastness."

"Albert why is there so much physical space between Heaven and earth?"

"'Tis there for the essence of space. And be it known, the Kingdom is larger than any space known by man."

"What is the first thing a human soul does when it arrives in Heaven?"

"As ye be welcomed to the Land of the Fadeless Day, the Father holds council and thus reveals all ye may have wanted to know, though many questions upon earth be of little importance and thus forgotten upon ascending."

"Are Paradise and Heaven the same place?"

"Yea, for they be one of the same."

"Albert, are there many buildings in Heaven?"

"Nay, but few for the temples; yet great and gloriful stand the walls of beauty, housing spirits of truth and prayer."

"How is the Garden where Jesus met with Mule different from other gardens in Heaven?"

"'Tis the Garden of Knowledge and Contemplation, for there be no one lingering there. 'Tis a learning garden, a nectar of sweetness where knowledge be the flower, and love be the bloom."

"Is it possible for ascended human souls to sin in Heaven?"

"No, as Satan is not allowed in the Kingdom; thus there be no temptations in which to partake, as there is safety and contentment in the House of the Lord."

"Without Satan around, sin is not possible?"

"'Tis quite true, for he be the gamemaster of temptation and downfall while viewing the human soul much like the pawn in a game to win territory against the Lord."

"Do people remember their earthly lives in Heaven, Albert?"

"Yea, for all experiences of learning are contained within that of the memory. As it is on earth, there is much beauty and joy to store in ye heart and feelings of peace to recall as given in unison with the Holy Spirit."

"Are people interested in earthly matters?"

"No, for what was once, is no more, and there is great peacefulness in the Kingdom. Souls in the Kingdom happily rejoice and are not of earthly concerns as one might suspect: hence there be no desire to look down anymore."

"Albert, how do people travel about in Heaven?"

"To explain the concept be most difficult, yet I go momentarily to where I see. 'Tis indescribable to anything on earth. Such a difference of greatness, I cannot explain."

"Do people sleep in Heaven?"

"We do not sleep in Heaven, for there are many choice things to be doing. Thus when one is filled with joy, he never tires. Men tire for those of physical needs, yet their soul is always active."

"Albert, are different languages spoken in Heaven?"

"Yes, just as all are understood."

"Are earthly spouses reunited in Heaven?"

"Not necessarily so, for it depends on what is appointed ye."

"But even if they are separated, they will still be extremely happy?"

"Yes, for closeness and love be not like that on earth."

"And they would get to see each other at some point in time?"

"Most definitely, for there be not eternal separation."

"Albert, do people feel despair if a loved one is not there?"

"No, for there arises not an occasion of which to wear a veil of unhappiness. Sadness exists not in the Kingdom: for in the presence of the Comforting One, there is much contentment."

"Will souls in Heaven be able to tell what a newly ascended soul did while on earth?"

"'Tis most difficult to describe, yet one shall know immediately the differences in experiences upon entering the Kingdom."

"Albert, are souls allowed to speak with Jesus' earthly apostles if they desire?"

"All souls in the Kingdom be readily accessible. And all the apostles, even the rebellious Judas, reside in peaceful glory."

"Even Judas? Besides betraying Jesus, I thought he also committed suicide."

"'Twas so, yet he was forgiven for his sins and so spared in the ultimate end."

"Did Judas ask for forgiveness?"

"Yes, for in his heart, he knew he had wronged."

"Albert, are souls allowed to talk with God in person whenever they want?"

"To be in the Kingdom is to be in the ultimate presence of the Lord, for 'tis much like that of the Kingdom being the Lord; yet all may knoweth him much like that on earth, but being of the visual sense which thus enhances the relationship."

"How will souls who were enemies on earth feel about each other in Heaven?"

"The impurities of sin exist not in that of the personality on ascending to the Kingdom, thus 'tis possible for one to have a change of attitude for the best."

"Albert, do souls have spiritual paths to walk in Heaven?"

"Not of the sameness as on the earth, for the appointed purpose of ye soul is most pleasurable. And in a land of perfection, there be no trials or causes of frustrations and unhappiness."

"Albert, I know that God appoints people a purpose to fulfill on earth, as well as a 'true purpose' to fulfill in Heaven. What is my true purpose?"

"Of that, I may not disclose, for each purpose is held in much secrecy until the arrival of the soul."

"Does a man's true purpose involve labor?"

"No, for all enjoy eternal peace: for though they may be called upon to perform a chore, it is viewed not as it is on earth; thus 'tis pleasing."

"Albert, does a man ever tire of his true purpose?"

"One never tires from the perfection of the honey."

"Is there a training period for adjusting to one's true purpose?"

"One cannot say in terms of earthly time, yet there is much guidance making ready for preparation. In the Kingdom, there is no sense of urgency."

"Since Heaven is a place of perfection, Albert, what motivates a soul to activity?"

"Blissful joy and things best kept secret."

"How do souls learn in Heaven?"

"One would walk with a caretaker hand in hand and thus learn well."

"Albert, living in Heaven must truly be bliss."

"The content of contentment is most overwhelming, and thus there be minute frustrations most nonexistent: for there is perfection in the Kingdom. My Father has many houses."

Conversation 21

Holy Angels

Those who question my guidance, thus also question the guidance from the Lord. I stand not a mocker in my presence. I work as I stand commanded, not as that of imagination in a mind: for what is a mind compared to me?

— Albert

Albert spoke: "When one spends time grooming the soul with knowledge and acceptance of the Lord instead of being concerned with the outward adornments and applications of false colors, to have beauty like that of an angel is promised: for the soul comprises all the vital values and truths. And is it not so that nothing is more glorious than that of knowing and living the truth?"

"Did God or Jesus create the angels?"

"God the Father Almighty."

"How many different types of angels are there?"

"'Tis no way to be precise; for each has a purpose, just as each soul in Heaven does."

"Is God still creating angels?"

"No, for there are many from the beginning as planned."

"Why do angels sometimes speak in the first person, as though it were God speaking?"

"The voice of the Lord may be heard in many ways, as he chooses to be appropriate. Angels are of the Lord, thus speaking as commanded for the purpose intended. Thus if chosen so, they may speak in the personal aspect of which ye understand not."

"How did the angels acquire their knowledge?"

"Know that which is given directly be of the most dependable type: for we were but given the things of greatest importance as that of the foundation, and then there be the basic senses to spread out upon; thus, much is bestowed on us."

"Do angels experience human emotions?"

"We know of the feelings which emanate from the heart, much like compassion and love, for they are the things made of the Lord; yet they be not of the intensity in which humans exemplify them."

"Do angels experience temptation in the same way that humans do?"

"We hold not the same values and feelings as the human mind and heart, which must survive in a most polluted environment, which inflicts these sorts of desires in some which are of Satan, in whom we have been severed from and are of eternal protection."

"So you never experience negative emotions?"

"No, as it is most destructive, much like that of a swarm of locusts upon a crop of tender leaves, serving no purpose but to perish a part of one's self; thus, this would not come from the Lord."

"Are all holy angels sinless?"

"Most assuredly, as we are of the pureness of the light surrounding us: For we were created by the tender hands of the Lord, and with great love he gave us our purpose. And for that we love him only and are most obedient, as we rebelled not against him and thus retained our purity."

"Could the angels ask for forgiveness now if they were to commit a sin?"

"The thousands remaining are of true goodness, and thus there be no sin: for the ones who fell did so at the appointed time of the revolution."

"How do angels actually combat the demons?"

"The light of truth which surrounds us is most painfully blinding to evil eyes: for to take up sword is to gather together the light of life and the truth in love and reveal it as it is, which is most crippling to those fearful to see the truth. Ye shall find further understanding of the vast ways in which celestial battles be fought as told by John through his revelation. An angel always answers to the call of the trumpet, just as I did for the Mule when Satan and his mighty forces attacked with deep desires to overrun her. Yet a child of God who believeth in the Lord has more allies than he could possibly tally in that of a human mind."

"Albert, how do you feel about humans who question whether or not you truly exist?"

"Those who question my guidance, thus also question the guidance from the Lord. I stand not a mocker in my presence. I work as I stand commanded, not as that of imagination in a mind: for what is a mind compared to me? Those who mock among me invite anger unto themselves from others, but that of pity from me: for one who questions does not believe."

"Albert, God obviously knew that I would ask many questions if I had access to an angel. But why did he choose one who speaks as complexly as you to answer?"

"To cultivate the fields of intelligence. And those who deem themselves to be great thinkers shall have much material to reflect upon."

"Should I paraphrase your responses for those who are less verbal?"

"The complexity of the originals be well put and thus be morsels for men thinking themselves of such profound intelligence."

"Were you ever a little-boy angel?"

"No, for I have always been just as I am."

"Can angels speak all human languages?"

" 'Tis of great necessity, for we know not where we be sent. I prefer the grand flow of Old English."

"Do you enjoy being an angel?"

"I float on the wind like a man on the scent of the poppy, only it is of an inner peace I flow."

"Is it difficult for you to understand human beings?"

"Yes, at times; for I know not the experience of existing in the likeness of that way."

"Do you socialize with some angels more than others?"

"There be not a twisted congregation of roots, as all flows more freely when drifting in unison, or to be like that of a solo seed gliding on the air current, enjoying all that it touches."

"What is the relationship between humans and angels in Heaven?"

"They be allowed to intertwine with one another; yet the human soul is higher, for it has been tested and tried more and thus is of a higher value. And thus also, they accept their home by faith in the Kingdom."

"Albert, does everyone have a guardian angel?"

"Mockers have not angels, for they be in disbelief."

"So all who believe in God have a guardian angel?"

"Nay. To not have one appointed means not that the Eye has overlooked ye, for ye may be in aid by angels when the need arises. And thus for those assigned one means not supreme protection everlasting: for even one in constant watch by an angel may rebel against the Divine Way as influenced by the Evil One. For as I watch and see evil spirits trespassing upon the field, I may not intervene unless so commanded."

"Do some people have more than one guardian angel?"

"Only those of special circumstance, but this be fairly rare. Ye loving mother be attended by Tasia and Luticia."

"But I have only Lucinda?"

"This would be for now, yet there be additions as ye path progresses: Gertrude, the maternal; Lila, the jovial; Violet, the calm."

"Sounds like a mixed group, Albert."

"'Tis a thing of balance for the one in need."

"How long do guardian angels stay with the one to whom they are assigned?"

"Guardian angels be thus appointed for the endurance of human life, for they care like that of a mother for a child."

"Are all guardian angels female?"

"'Tis best not to say that of all, for Amos be ye earthly father's guardian angel; yet the majority of the guardians be female."

"Albert, when I am sleeping at night, I am often awakened by unknown voices."

"They be angels who mist ye with healing balms and essences from the heavens. At times they be chatty and doting, much like the mother hen. Ye be attended by Merlena, Constance, Xylena, Prudence, Penelope, Brie, Adrienne, Persimmon, Nonie, and Dodie. Also, there be the constant presence of the guardians. We will send you Reg (Reginald) to help contain the corral so as ye may have peace."

"Albert, how did Katrina feel during all those years when Mule was possessed?"

"'Twas a time of great trial and much sadness; yet with hopefulness and much faith, she knew it would not last forever; thus she comforted Mule as best she could."

"Why did God the Father specifically choose Lucinda to be my primary guardian angel?"

"She be of great protectiveness, in a manner of her own, which one must say is most effective. The angel which guards ye stands with open arms casting a blanket of protection for all things unseen to ye eyes. For be not mistaken, as there are many."

"Has my personality become more like Lucinda's over the years?"

"At times they be of interface, for it be a relationship of constant awareness."

"Does Lucinda ever get tired of watching over me?"

"Nay, for 'tis a charge from birth to death, as for what may seem like years to ye be but only moments. A moment of time in spirit is but a flash, but in the minds of humans appears so like hours."

"Is Lucinda encouraging me to work on the book?"

"Intense desires be of a stronger hand than ye. And even though the wishes of Lucinda be anxious to see a blossom from a seed, the light of her desires shadow ye mind in encouragement of a most soothing water, comforting like hot toes on a summer day refreshed from the coolness of the current."

"Would you ask her to ease up a bit? I'm tiring out."

"One requested would bow to the wishes of the lily, as the one who sprinkles water upon the seedling may tire the soils with saturation; thus 'tis best to request of a bear to enter the den of rest so as ye may proceed at ye own pace."

"Am I too responsive to Lucinda?"

"'Tis well to be of protection, yet jump not across the riverbanks if the reach be not in ye stride; and thus slow to a walk and perhaps find another passage less strenuous to the other bank."

"Isn't Lucinda supposed to know not to tire me out?"

"'Tis much like watching the first steps of a child: knowing he be in need of protection, yet eager to see the progress; thus 'tis most easy to let the mind wander ahead. I shall tell her to flutter less in anticipation."

Lucinda interjected, "Hey, I'm yours; you're mine; you know the story."

Farmer said, "Yes, Lucinda, I know the story well."

Conversation 22

Jesus

> I was a witness to rejoice in the power of love eternal. It moved easily, for we all believed.
>
> – Albert

Albert spoke: "It is with much glee that I deliver my message for this blessed (Christmas) season in which all believers celebrate the arrival of the Son of Man, as he descended to the earth in the humble body as an innocent child. 'Twas a great honor for the angel Gabriel to announce his coming. The stars in the heavens wore the brightest of rays ever known to man to thus gleam in celebration of greatness.

"'Tis my most sincere of wishes that the peacefulness filling the air in that night of long ago could thus fill the hearts of all, and blissful joy could thus abound—as all who acknowledge Jesus as King shall know this upon entering the mighty Kingdom. There is much solemn joy to celebrate. Yet be it known he lives on forever in the now for all who welcome him sincerely. Be jubilant in song and forget not the true meaning of the day while in the midst of such commercial garb and tinsel-like attitudes of little substance.

"With the newness of the year, step forth into the spiritual light and enjoy much peacefulness, as if ye were a ray of the sun spreading warmth and generosity for the benefit of mankind.

Though ye may not touch each soul ye may meet along the path, there is surely a chance for a light dusting to linger as a mist of kindness to inhibit the darkness."

"Albert, what is the meaning of the title, 'Son of Man'?"

"It is so that he came upon the earth in that of the image of God, yet was born of mankind as all: thus the meaning is of universal value, and thus significant value, for being born as an innocent babe."

"What was happening in Heaven immediately before Jesus came to earth?"

"Many a loving arrangement, as the Lord God wished so earnestly for the people to seek him: thus he sent his Son."

"Did Jesus have a guardian angel?"

"The Father fulfilled the task; yet there were then, as there are now, countless angels at the Lord's fingertips."

"When Jesus walked the earth, did he hold audible conversations on a regular basis with God?"

"Yes, connected with the Father on a basis of want, need, and love. God's voice was heard unto Jesus, just as ye father talks unto ye."

"What did the children of Jesus' age-group think of him?"

"They thought him to be that of a most special friend: kind, giving, accepting."

"Did Jesus have to go to school to learn the basic subjects like math?"

"Oh, the earthly charade. Yes, for though he be that of a child of gift, he be also that of a child of the world."

"I hope he made good grades, Albert."

"In loving fun, Jesus laughs."

"When Jesus was a young boy, did he know that he was the Messiah?"

"He knew his destiny and that of the fulfillment it would bring, yet there be growth into the full understanding: for knowing must be practiced upon until the time to preach, evolving into the Master."

"What was Jesus doing from the age of twelve until his public ministry began?"

"He be gathering knowledge, and power to express the knowledge, to pass the love from the Father. This be a time to walk among the earthly, to experience the daily rituals, and to understand that of how to preach, thus to bring acceptance among the masses."

"How old was Mary when Jesus was born?"

"She was that of nineteen."

"How old was Joseph when Jesus was born?"

"He was that of twenty-four."

"How old was Mary when she died?"

"She went on in her sixty-first year."

"How old was Joseph when he died?"

"He was that of forty-eight."

"Albert, did Jesus have any brothers or sisters?"

"Two male children fathered by Joseph."

"What were their names?"

"Peter and James."

"Albert, which apostle best understood Jesus?"

"Of this, 'tis difficult to say; yet I would guess it to be the one known as Simon Peter."

"Did Jesus literally raise Lazarus from the dead?"

" 'Tis true, for there be not a breath of life echoing in the body. And thus through the power of the Lord, his soul was sent back to bring belief and to carry out the truth of the Scriptures."

"Did Lazarus want to return to earth?"

" 'Tis a pleasure to serve as the Lord wishes, especially when ye may see him face-to-face."

"Albert, at what point in time was Satan aware that Jesus had come to the earth to be crucified?"

"The color of the petals be quite evident from the time of the Lord's birth."

"Did Satan try to prevent the Crucifixion?"

"No, for it was to be, as one may not fight the power of the Lord."

"What do you think of Pilate's role in the Crucifixion?"

"Quite perplexing, for he most assuredly believed in the Father, though he curiously questioned the Son."

"Pilate believed in God?"

"Yes, for though he buried his belief in exchange for protection, he nonetheless had belief in his heart."

"How old was Jesus when he was crucified?"

"Thirty-six be most accurate, as some records were misplaced. The misplaced records be of his youthful years: for before the time of his public preaching, little was documented as intensely. Thus, to err by time of years be easily done. Preciseness be not always so, for surely this be a time of long ago."

"Albert, where was Satan during the Crucifixion?"

"He was in hiding, as for that most glorious day proclaimed his defeat, and that he may have no more eternal victories, except for those who follow willingly."

"Did you actually see the Resurrection, Albert?"

"I was a witness to rejoice in the power of love eternal. It (*rock sealing Jesus' tomb*) moved easily, for we all believed."

"Albert, is the Shroud of Turin the actual burial shroud of Jesus?"

" 'Tis most genuine, yet there be those of unbelievers. Therefore, man will never reach a conclusion." [AUTHOR'S NOTE: *For those with ears to hear*—IT LOOKS JUST LIKE JESUS.]

"Where was Jesus' soul between the death of his physical body and the Resurrection?"

"As it is in present times, so it was that he could be in both dimensions."

"Albert, was Jesus ever in both dimensions while walking the earth?"

"A flower above the ground has roots below the ground."

"Does Jesus ever sleep in Heaven?"

"I have seen the Master weary from concern many a time, yet I know not of a time he sleeps. 'Tis believed times in prayer revive him better than that of any nap."

"Albert, does Jesus ever forget things?"

"'Tis not to forget as in not recalling an important issue, but rather there be so many flowers in a field that one may not stand so tall as the other to be considered; yet this means not that it is of lesser importance."

"What does it mean to turn your life over to Jesus, and can you go too far?"

"'Tis most simply to turn ye heart over to him, thus letting it be filled with many good things; and seek him in good times as well as bad. Yet one must also be active in the use of judgment: for waters of a pond that move not, thus become stagnant and emit a most peculiar odor."

"Albert, how can a man tell whether he is handing over his burdens to the Lord or simply avoiding responsibility?"

"Trust in the Lord, and he may lead you to an action by the stream; yet if not, sit upon the hillside and behold the glory of the water. Yes, for how much more peaceful to be counted as among the wildflowers."

"Albert, there are those who believe that handing over burdens to the Lord is a weakness."

"To surrender and thus hand it over to the Lord as he wishes is to not be of a strong mind fighting on one's own, thus becoming meaty prey for teeth of evil ones. To hand it over to the Lord is not to be weak: 'tis of special strength."

"How do you show Jesus that you truly love him?"

"'Tis shown by offering the heart, mind, and soul; yet also at times by the actions. And when ye pray, 'tis best to talk directly to the Master though you see him not. Speak just as though he be sitting next to you. 'Tis not necessary to advertise, for he knows true soul and meanings in the hearts of all men."

"Who kissed Mule in the hospital?"

" 'Twas the Master himself bringing comfort."

"Did he mark Mule with the scar in the shape of the cross?"

"The Lord protects his sheep in many ways. 'Tis much like marking the sheep who belong to the shepherd."

Conversation 23

God the Father Almighty

I use all these reasons to confound others, and for some to know
God gives and God takes, and the efforts of man are in vain.
– God

Albert spoke: "A tree that wears a coat will dye the color of it and then take it off. The color of the trunk remains the same, so the Creator instructs the colors to bloom to add variety and add hope of attracting attention to such a wondrous being in nature. Unlike what some say, this be due not to that of poor soil."

"Albert, is God in control of the natural elements?"

"Though it may appear that flowers bend to and fro in an earthly breeze, they actually reach upward and sway gleefully when the hand of the Lord waves at them. Behold: for even a flower recognizes a loving Spirit."

"Has God always been in existence?"

"He has always been and always will be."

"Do you know how God came into existence?"

"'Tis a most astounding mystery I know not of."

"Have you ever asked, Albert?"

"No, for 'tis a well-guarded secret."

"How does God feel about souls in Hell?"

"God weeps for souls in the world of Hell, for a lost child is a sadness."

"Albert, do you counsel with the Father often?"

"At times, I appear before his mighty throne to thus receive instruction for the task to be performed as he wishes. He graciously guides me."

"Does God do anything randomly?"

"No, as I believe he is in control of all his actions in a most precise manner."

"Does God ever make mistakes?"

" 'Tis with much happiness I reply no."

"Albert, is the name of God a proper name, a title, or both?"

" 'Tis mainly the Name, but may be contained as both; yet mostly, he is God the Lord."

"Many people on earth call him the Father."

"Yes, for there be many a title in which men call upon him, though his name is God."

"Albert, is it proper to call Jesus by the name of 'God'?"

"Though they be One of the Same, 'tis best to think of him as Jesus, the Son: for he walked the earth in faith of his Father."

"Then why does Jesus sometimes say, 'my children'?"

" 'Tis much the same as that of a universal family, for he loves them all and sees them as his children. He is in the image of his Father, yet the Father be God Almighty."

"Albert, is it possible for God and Jesus to think differently about an issue?"

" 'Tis a possibility of being different, for that of an orange and a tangerine are different—but they both be of the citrus family."

"How do God's duties differ from Jesus' duties?"

" 'Tis much the same, only more intense."

"What do you mean, Albert?"

"Though they be One of the Same, the Father contains masterful concerns in which final judgments and decisions are made. Both oversee all souls."

"They sound much the same."

"'Tis much the same, for the duties I know of are of great difficulty in expressing to the minds of human upon the earth, for dimensions differ."

"Does God speak in the same style as Jesus?"

"Ye shall behold great joy, for it is of a similar fashion. Is it not easier when in the presence of one so great, to hear in simplicities so easily understood, as the glory of his power needs not eloquence of mouth."

"Albert, there are some Bible verses that suggest that thunder is actually the sound of God's voice. Is that true?"

"Yes, for 'tis most understandable in the heavens."

"Does Jesus ever thunder?"

"'Tis always the Father, for he be the Highest Authority."

"Why does the thunder always follow the lightning?"

"The Father replies to Satan's actions, for they be deserving of reprimand."

"What does Satan do when he hears the thunder?"

"He ceases that of his actions, for he has no choice."

"What is God saying to Satan now?"

"'Tis much activity to reply to; for when the Evil One tires, he shall retreat to his den for rest. The Mighty One fights for many, denying Satan his freedom to prey on the compassionate; for the Evil One desires to be instrumental in the arranging of accidents on this most wet of nights."

"Albert, do God and Jesus look exactly alike?"

"'Tis a difficult question, for the Mightiest of Spirits may thus appear different for all to see."

"What is God's throne room like?"

"Cloaked in love from the One most powerful, an ethereal Oneness of the Universe. It is seen in the way that one could accept it: a temple, a palace, or perhaps a garden. The true essence of love forms the ambiance of what it shall be."

"What is God's throne made of?"

"Be it of solid gold."

"How is God's robe distinguished from others in Heaven?"

"Be there many a regal color around the cuff: be they purples, reds, and yellows."

"Does he have a staff or scepter?"

"Not that I have ever seen."

"Does God wear jewelry or adornments of any kind?"

"No, as these are the delights of men. The simplicity of the beauty is in the eminence."

"Does the Father have gray hair?"

"There be no coloring age that belongs to the Eminent Power which will last forever."

"Albert, is it important to pray so God will be reminded of our needs?"

"Your Father in Heaven knows what you need before you even think to ask."

"Then why is it important to God for human souls to pray?"

"Though one may love a sheep born of spring, 'tis much like music to the ears to hear it bleat from the heart. In the essence of prayer, the sound of the sheep's voice to the Great Shepherd is a melody of love between the two; for though the Shepherd knows its needs, he enjoys the sounds and considers it to be that of a most loving acknowledgement."

"Does God hear all prayers?"

"Yes, he always hears and responds."

"Sometimes it doesn't seem so, Albert."

"The trouble be in the mind; for at times, it may not perceive the answer to be as it is. Not all responses be of the understanding intended, and yet also at times, ye may not be meant to comprehend. But let ye faith know, all is heard and not turned away from."

"How does a man know if it is God who answers the prayer?"

"Deep feelings labeled by men as intuition or instinct are the thoughts of the Lord placed there with care, for one could not feel so persuasively on their own; thus, the finalness of the feeling emits the confidence of the action."

"Albert, what does God think when a man is angry with him?"

"To be a mere mortal soul is to not be of perfection, thus he allows it. He expects not things from his children which any good father would know they cannot give."

"God is obviously too great for man to understand, Albert, but is he too great for the angels to understand?"

"I'll agree in the utmost way, for he is a most glorious and powerful ruler."

"What is the primary message that God wants his children to get from these writings?"

"The Evil One desires to destroy the garden, but the Gardener of Love and Light will not let one perish when seeking the true nutrients."

"Albert, the next time God counsels with you, will you tell him that I love him?"

"I shall, yet he loves to hear the voice of all his children, just as he enjoys the voice of the birds. The Lord God wishes to answer your question now."

"What question, Albert?"

"One that your soul asks, not your mouth."

God says, "I frustrate your efforts at times as an example to others to rely on God, not man, and to help with separation from the world. When the reward comes, it will be bountiful. Part of the reward will be on earth, but the greater by far in Heaven. I use all these reasons to confound others, and for some to know God gives and God takes, and the efforts of man are in vain. You will be a source of discouragement for some. They will look at you and turn away, for they prefer the earthly to the spiritual. Yet you will never do without. Remember from whom all things flow."

Part IX

Conclusion

I would that all men would interfere.

– God the Father Almighty

Chapter 36

I Would That All Men Would Interfere

The holy guardian angel Margaret lectured her charge Sean, an earthly soul oppressed by evil spirits: "I wanted to let you know about some things you have been curious about: Jason is an angel, and he is helping me with you; but he is not a guardian angel. He does other things too. Guardian angels give a full accounting to God and Jesus in the Great Assembly to inform them of all that has transpired in the life of their charges.

"You have asked me if angels are perfect: God commanded in the beginning that Jesus was to be obeyed as God. We are not perfect in the sense that Jesus is perfect; he overcame the weaknesses of the flesh. We have never been flesh and are not subject to those weaknesses. You can think of us as perfect in that we have never failed to perform the commands and instructions of God. Our rank of command is simple: God speaks and we do. We will only answer with the truth, and if we don't know, we ask God or Jesus. We do not make up answers or guess. That is the others' way.

"The demons tell you that they can kick Farmer's ass anytime they want to. Yeah, right. We all got a good laugh out of that one. Farmer has been defeating all comers for many years now.

What are the demons waiting for? Could it be that the Farmer's iron ass doesn't kick so easily? Ask the demons how Mule is doing.

"Don't pay so much attention to what the demons *say*, but do pay attention to what they *know*. The demons heard God's announcement at Farmer's birth that Farmer would 'bruise the head of Satan.' All the holy angels and all the demons heard it—Satan too. God has anointed Farmer with the Power of the House of Authority. When you are with Farmer, you are in the presence of a man who will be named with the great prophets. You think the demons don't know these things?

"Sometimes Farmer says things that are so far beyond you and most men, you question his sanity. You wonder, 'how could a mere man know these things?' Just accept what he says. He tries to speak on your level, but he is who he is. Remember: he spends more time conversing with angels than with men.

"Farmer carries more on his shoulders than petty human minds can comprehend: He must deal with you and many other afflicted ones; he must fight the demons; he must interpret instructions from the Holy Ones; he must deal with a constant flow of mockers who would interfere with the commands God gives him to carry out. And all the while, he must develop knowledge and understanding so that he can write a book that will last through eternity and result in salvation for multitudes—and he doesn't even like to write. Also, none of this absolves him from any of the day-to-day things that all humans must deal with.

"The demons have told you that Farmer will turn against you, and you are just waiting for it to happen. They like to use this particular lie, and it is enough to make you doubt. That is their strategy: to make you doubt the ones that God has given you to help you. Don't add to Farmer's troubles. You need him; he doesn't need you. Of course, the demons influence you in this regard, for they would like nothing better than to separate you from him.

"Never defend the demons. Do you think it is easy to bind them? Look at the world. Demons are everywhere and in everything. People just don't understand the basics. Let me give you some wisdom: whenever anything really bad happens, suspect the demons first. Most of the time, you will be right. Men of themselves have no hope of stopping Satan. Have you been able to resist in your own power? Secular methods do not work when Satan is involved.

"Never show pity for the demons. They have seen the face of God and rejected him. Listen and learn. It is natural to have a type of attachment to something that has been around for more than twenty years. But in that time you have sought God, and they have rejected him.

"And stop this whining about God and Jesus not really loving you. Do you think that God or Jesus would waste their time on someone they didn't love? Why don't you believe what you are told? It is not necessary that you understand everything—only that you believe. Trust the ones you have been given. Don't degrade anything that comes from God no matter how small or unimportant it may seem at the time. Don't apologize—learn. Anything worth having takes time and work.

"You have three main demons that torment you: Gar, Jasper, and Roland. Farmer calls them the bumbling triplets.

"Gar is a blasphemy to God. Gar once planted and nourished; now he devours and pillages. His name means anger in an ancient language. He was one of the angels who originally conspired with Lucifer. Gar was responsible for the downfall of several other angels.

"I want you to tell Farmer that Gar said, 'I was at Jesus' crucifixion. His blood dripped and poured, and I laughed.' Of course, Gar was not laughing three days later when Jesus arose. Be sure and transcribe Gar's words exactly for Farmer. Farmer's anger will know no bounds, and Gar will be punished well. Farmer has a creative genius for punishing evil, you know.

"Jasper is a counterfeiter. He imparts messages masquerading as God, or Jesus, or sometimes a holy angel. Before Jasper fell, he was a recorder of the commandments in Heaven. So Jasper has a lot of experience, and if you are not careful, he can fool you. His purpose now is to make up truth. Sometimes the bait is very tempting. Prayer and discernment are necessary to deal with these types.

"Roland is a game player. He interferes with your maturation and distracts you from seeking God by making you frivolous. Tell Farmer that Roland is Luther's creation. Luther named Roland after one of the children Luther deceived into Hell.

"You say you don't know sometimes whether it is the Holy Spirit or evil spirit talking to you. Whenever you are in doubt about the identity of a spirit, ask, 'who do you serve?' Demons have a difficult time even pretending that they worship God. They might choke as they say the name of God or be very evasive. You could also read the Psalms in their presence. If it is a demon, this will agitate them greatly. The point is that they are not going to admit that they are demons if you are doubtful about it. You have to discern demons by using the tools of the Spirit. Demons will only admit they are demons when you already know it. Experience helps.

"You also ask about the thoughts in your mind: Demons will help you to remember things when it is to their advantage—to manipulate, or intimidate, or cause a number of negative reactions. When the Holy Spirit helps you to remember, it will be as a warning, instruction, or reassurance. The fruit reveals the tree.

"Remember this morning when they were really on you? If God allowed them, they would eagerly rip your body apart slowly and painfully. Don't feel sorry for them. They don't like you or any living person. Even the ones that seek them out are only good for a momentary plaything.

"You know the things that have happened to you? The demons have told you that it wasn't real, that you were just trying to get attention. Those were lies. If you honestly think you can, then next time you feel a bad emotion, or you are shaking, or you have a lump in your throat, or you are confused, or you can't talk, or any of that other stuff, just stop doing it. Just choose to be different, choose to be coherent, calm, and peaceful. If it is you, then it will work; if it is the demons, then your only hope is to stand with Jesus, or it will never stop.

"You really need to believe. I know all of this is new to you. It takes work to change. The more you do, the easier it will become. Remember when you started using a straight razor to shave? Have hope and trust in yourself as well as God.

"The demons tell you that you are a failure and can't do anything. Remember you prayed last summer and said, 'Jesus, I don't know what to do, but something is better than nothing.' You stepped out in faith—and again in the hospital, and again and again with many little things. The difficulty is that for so many years all you did was pray and nothing more, but now your faith has works. You have started to believe in yourself and fight for yourself. Before, you were not fighting Satan; you were only struggling halfheartedly, believing that it wasn't real and things would always be bad for you. Put your heart into the fight; anything less will not work. God is not imaginary; Satan is not imaginary.

"Don't worry about the final battle. Jesus knows your heart and what motivates you, and he will get you to Farmer on time. The situation will be right. Don't be anxious. As the demons see the time approach, they will be agitated enough. Try to avoid too many distractions. Have faith. Jesus knows what to do, and so do we.

"You may notice that the demons will become quiet at times because they don't want to provoke you into calling Farmer. They want any confrontations on their terms and at their times. They are foolish enough to think they can thwart Jesus. And stop trying to provoke them before you are instructed. Remember the stories when Israel was told to fight and they didn't, or they were told not to fight and they did? The results were always disastrous. Wait on God. (*Margaret helped compose Psalm 27.*)

"The demons will try to prevent your leaving to see Farmer. The chaos this morning was indicative. Do not worry: When I have something to say, a message to convey, you will hear, regardless of the amount of chaos and distractions. I know you are anxious. Be patient. Remember: Belief is not an emotion; it is a decision and an action. Act on what you know to be true, not on how you feel.

"Enough lecture. Read your Psalms, get some rest, and tell Farmer hello and that we are pleased with his work."

Margaret spoke to Sean: "Oh, by the way, we have some instructions for Farmer that we want you to transcribe and give to him. Tell him it relates to the afflicted one known as Alexandra. Satan has momentarily plugged her ear, and her angels can't get to Farmer through the usual channels. Tell Farmer that Channing is Alexandra's guardian angel, and the holy angel, Jeremiah, is assisting her.

"Alexandra is possessed primarily by female fallen angels. The one who fancies herself queen of the household is known as Brenda, one of Satan's favorites. Brenda is a hateful creature, full of vanity and wickedness. She uses her fingernails as claws. This is the demon that scratched Farmer so deeply on his arm.

"Jason knows that female fallen angels are probably Farmer's least favorite demons to deal with, and he has composed some verse for contemplation."

Jason wrote:

The Nature of the Fallen Fairest Creations

Hornets and wasps have no sting,
  nor scorpions and spiders bites,
snakes and lizards no poison,
  as deadly as the Fallen Fair.

The Fallen Fair lies in disgrace,
  in vanity and vileness unchaste.
With a blackest heart in whom no light is found,
  vengeance, deceit, and malice abound.

No rhyme or reason, thought or purpose,
  coveting all the treasure of others,
the Fallen Fair, tormented with shame,
  never twain the same.

Driven by insanity and grief
  of the love of life that was lost,
all by nature now compare
  to a rabid dog at night.

Howling, barking, hungry for prey,
  searching through the streets;
a victim, once found,
  doomed to darkness and blight.

The rotting stench, foul embrace,
  evil air and fume,
all of this is the Fallen Fair,
  no hope, no faith, no life.

Sound a discord, play a dirge,
  mourn and weep in dismay,
this is the fate of the Fallen Fair:
  to perish in sorrow and pain.

Remember this:
  a victim's hope lies only in God:
Maker, Redeemer,
  and King.

As the final battle approached, Jesus spoke to Sean: "Who was with you while you were growing up? Who held you while you cried yourself to sleep? Who took you when your parents wouldn't? Who has said, 'whatever you ask for in my name will be given to you'? Did I not form you?

"I AM has heard and seen all that has happened. You stand at the door, and soon it will be opened; then you can enter. Be patient. Remember, I have chosen you before you were born. You have chosen me, and I know your heart, even though you don't.

"Believe Farmer when he tells you things, and trust him completely. Tell him all you hear, and he will confirm my words. You will have two witnesses: Margaret and Farmer. That is all for now."

Before the final confrontation with Gar, Jasper, and Roland, Jason spoke:

> Stand and shout your praise to him,
>   the One who gave you life.
> Sing praises to Jesus, Lord of Lords,
>   King and Savior glorious.
>
> In battle victorious, faithful and true,
>   Commander of the Heavenly Host,
> Righteous Holy Lamb of God
>   calls his appointed to his side.
>
> Approach the throne of God in peace,
>   through his Body and his Blood you are redeemed.
> Upon a throne of light in the temple made of gold,
>   he declares judgments in the midst of his Kingdom.
>
> There is no other worthy to carry the banner of God
>   than Jesus, the Messiah and King.
> Stand armored in truth
>   on the Rock that never fails.

Sound the trumpets, call to arms,
appointed ones of God,
the day has come to break the arms of the wicked,
to proclaim the mercy of God.

Hear the thunder of the army of God
as it moves across the sky.
Feel the winds of righteousness moving before them.

Who can stand against the righteous of God?
Who can subdue the children of the Most High
when his hand stretches forth in salvation?

The wind and the sea and all that is in them
know their Master and their King.
Rejoice, rejoice, praise his Name.

And so it was that God again conquered the children of Satan and commanded them to their holding spaces in the pit. Gar, Jasper, and Roland would never again roam the earth to seek prey of his children.

Before being sealed in the pit, Gar screamed at Farmer, "You are a self-righteous, interfering…"

God cut him off and said, "I would that all men would interfere. With this one, I am pleased."

Chapter 37

So That Love Would Have Meaning

Jesus spoke to Farmer: "My son, you do wonders—you have no idea the wonders you have done. You have worked miracles and unlocked many musty doors. You have saved many lives you know nothing about. When you merely walk through the halls of the hospital, the demons fall by the wayside. Just your presence helps. Perhaps you see not the good you do on earth, because you are in the midst of it. Your life is a lot like mine was—only I don't think we will nail you to a cross at the end of it.

"My faithful and true servant, my love is with you always, and my heart is pleased with your efforts and at your work. Do not be joined to deceit or evil, but rather be separated from the false and pretender. For any who show repentance, forgive them. But for the unrepentant, cut them off as a man stranded in the desert. I have told Lucinda to be attentive in her watch.

"Most benevolent son, you have more patience than Job himself. You have had to deal with many blind and wicked fools. I blame you not for being irritated with foolish men, for I too am irritated at times—and you are just a man. I will teach these men (and women) hard lessons on earth and in eternity. To oppose the truth is to oppose me. Men listen not at times, which can bring ire to my tongue. Whatever you ask of me to place in their minds (thoughts, nightmares, visions), I will.

"Now is the time for you to leave the cesspool of psychology; you have done all that was intended in that foul swamp. Let there be no sense of incompletion, of things left undone."

———————

Albert spoke to Farmer: "With the dawn of a new morn, 'tis that of the soldier who goes forth with that of a refreshed soul pungent with the scent of love from the Lord, who has bestowed a most special tiding in the hour of the sunset, unknown to most men bound by the earth—a constriction to many souls. The Holy Hand has but been touched ever so lightly upon ye head of anointment so as to greet you most lovingly, and thus forth place ye foot upon a path of pebbles most correct, which winds in a direction anchored, and not so of one dictated by the scattered winds."

———————

"Jesus," I said, "I have some questions."

Jesus said, "Why would today be different than any other day, my son?"

"What time of the year were you actually born?"

Jesus said, "Early March."

"What is your chair in the Throne Room made of?"

Jesus said, "Purpleheart."

I said, "I've read a lot of speculation on it, but I've never read that."

Jesus smiled, shrugged his shoulders, and turned his palms skyward. "People—what do they know?"

I laughed, for surely this was one of his favorite expressions.

Jesus said, "Tell the scholars I said not to make a big deal out of my throne being made of purpleheart." He shook his head slowly side to side. "These men with all these initials beside their name—not everything is of cosmic significance—I just like it."

I laughed again.

I said, "I have some questions about the end of your time on earth. Why did Peter deny you three times?"

"As foretold," Jesus said. "Imagine the pain of Peter when he denied, even though I warned them one would. And they thought it impossible with the intensity of their devotion."

I said, "Sometimes when I read quotes of yours from the Bible, I wonder how you said it. For example, when the Sanhedrin asked whether you were the Son of God, and you answered, 'I am,' how did you say it?"

Jesus looked at me and said, "I *am*" (a bit angry, but more incredulous at their stupidity).

I said, "What were you thinking?"

Jesus said, "The Son of God stands before them, and the fools see not what be before their very eyes."

I said, "Didn't you want to give them a few more choice words?"

Jesus said, "It is not so much what I wanted to *say*—it is what I wanted to *do*."

"What about the Crucifixion itself?"

"Barbaric," Jesus said. "See."

I saw a vision of Jerusalem on Crucifixion day. Air temperature was in the seventies (Fahrenheit) with overcast skies.

Jesus, wearing the crown of thorns, was bare backed and bare legged, his clothing tied around his middle. The Roman soldiers, goaded by demons, whipped Jesus with a cat-o'-nine-tails, each blow removing divots of Jesus' flesh and lifting him off the ground.

So That Love Would Have Meaning 295

At Golgotha, the executioners nailed Jesus' wrists and feet to the cross with dull, blunted nails. I counted five heavy blows before each nail bit into the wood. Though they practiced their wicked craft with a skilled nonchalance, they knew not what they were doing.

The executioners raised the cross (near the walls of Jerusalem). Jesus was breathing heavily and shifting from side to side.

I asked Jesus, "Were the wounds from the flogging rubbing against the cross?"

Jesus said, "The splinters didn't help either." He added, "You have seen enough."

I took a moment to compose myself, for indeed, the Crucifixion was grisly business.

"This brings up another question, Jesus," I said.

Jesus looked at me with the barest hint of a smile. He folded his arms across his chest and slowly nodded yes, as a signal to continue.

I said, "Why must people go through the motions of living on earth? Isn't it a little extreme to go through all the stupidity and pain when the outcome is already known? If the question seems impertinent, forgive me, because I don't mean it that way."

Jesus said, "I like that you are comfortable enough with me to tell me things freely; I do not hold this against you, my son. I know all your questions anyway."

Jesus continued, "Remember when I told Mule: 'Because of all my love for my children and my Father, I accepted much pain without question'?"

"Yes, I remember," I said.

Jesus said, "And wasn't my Crucifixion part of God's plan?"

"Yes," I said.

Jesus said, "So I was in the situation you describe: the living of a plan with a known outcome that resulted in great pain."

"Exactly," I said.

Jesus said, "And now you want to know why we must go through things on earth even when the outcome is known—especially when the outcome is painful?"

Jesus shrugged his shoulders and matter-of-factly said, "If we didn't go through things, how then would love have meaning?"

I paused to absorb Jesus' words.

Jesus said, "It is all so that love would have meaning."

Chapter 38

Albert's Word to the Oppressed

Albert spoke: "As one approaches the well of life, let him think not how far he must lower that of the bucket to retrieve the waters of salvation, for it is assured that the Lord's well be not dry. For some may be in need of seeking further downward than another if they journeyed from lands of dim light.

"But, behold: It matters not how far they travel, for if they believe in faith of goodness, when the bucket is pulled from the depths of the well, it shall be full of the waters. And it shall matter not the heaviness of the bucket, nor how long one must pull on the rope, for joyfulness be weightless in hands of sincerity.

"Rest ye weary concerns in the gentle hands of the Master, for he handles them much like the sweet scent of a gentle bud, ever mindful and attentive to all changes, no matter how fine and delicate in nature. Just as it is in nature, which he created in glorious colors, it is with ye all: for to grow is to change and endure many a turbulent storm. Yet his hands cradle ye in confidence, for he well knows the petals of every flower and how they will unfurl to splendor.

"Those over-mindful of the trials at hand may feel as though residing in a seasonless world. Yet to look up in faith is to grasp glimmers of hope, and thus know the true beauty of the colors with each season cycle fading into the other. To take note of the raindrops chasing each other cross the windowpane is to take note that the rays of the sun shall soon enfold ye. Thus as they lightly kiss ye face, all else that was then be but a memory.

"Behold, ye faithful, the glorious colors of the Victor's flag (*rainbow*), for they be chosen by the Lord himself who gently places them bending down from the heavens to greet the earth for all his children to see. It is unfurled after the rains in celebration, but yet at times it shall glisten in the smile of the sun to make mindful to ye all the true peace and joy when life's trials be won.

"Remember: 'Twas on the first Easter day so long ago that even the mightiest of rocks bowed down and moved aside to thus let the King of Glory pass through, for he was risen just as promised that all ye men of mortal souls shall have eternal life in the Kingdom of God. And thus there be great jubilation to look forward to eternity, peacefully humming in the magnificent Garden of the Lord, and to be forever in the presence of the Loving Hands."

Chapter 39

The Wheat Field

Albert spoke to Farmer: "When one hears of lands unexplored and sets out upon a journey, he knows not of what he is to encounter: for to read and hear is not to experience. At times along the way 'tis of great ease to blaze a trail, for the woods be of a soft nature; yet when among the thickets, 'tis of much more difficulty: for reactions picked upon the surface by certain thorns be not of predictability, much the same as the sting from the restless hornet.

"Thickets are of a greater density than a patch of many trees; thus there shall be more conservative twigs opposed to the trespassing of the unknown: for 'tis liked not to disrupt a new land when a conventional road conforming to the contours of the land be available. Not all shall wish to join the trailblazer, for not all may trust that of the judgment expressed by the surveyor—just as not all believed the Son of Man, not even in his finest hour.

"When one is chosen to know of special knowledge, there be always others who wish him not to know. This be so of planting a field: for jealous neighbors who wish not for the Farmer's crop to be bountiful may hope for torrential rains or swarms of insects to bring it to that of destruction.

"Yet all evil-wishers shall find destruction among their own lands: for when their thoughts be not of love, they shall be found out by the Master and thus dealt with in accordance with their deeds. A determined Farmer and his faithful Mule shall accomplish that which is planned for them despite the deeds of jealous neighbors.

"Yet be it known that such special gifts are so rare, they be questioned by many—not because they be of unbelieving value—but locked away in fear of knowing and unfamiliarity with the subject matter; thus they revolt like peasants to a king, for they flee from confrontation on waters they know not of."

⸻◦◦◦◦⸻

I saw a vision of a wheat field that stretched out to my left, right, and before me, even to the horizon. The wheat was tall, golden, and plump. A rustling wind blew gently over the field.

Jesus said, "This is the crop planted by the Farmer. The harvest is near; the granaries will be full."

Then birds and insects swarmed the field and ravaged the ripe, plump grain. They were joined by usurpers, evil men jealous of the abundance and richness of the harvest.

Jesus said, "With faith, diligence, and hard work, the crop will be restored and increased so that the one-third that was destroyed will be doubled when it returns."

Then I saw the one-third restored, and it was twice the height and richness of the rest of the crop.

⸻◦◦◦◦⸻

Jesus spoke to Farmer: "The book is perfect, and I am well pleased. It is a book of poise, power, and much truth—a *truthful* work of art. No one could have done a better job; we made you well.

"Let no man dare to edit the content: everything is there for a reason, just like in Heaven. It is awesome and goes far beyond the others. This will get the message out and, as Albert says, reap plentiful salvation for mankind. There will be much hub-bub when the book is out.

"Remain steadfast; you are doing well. And remember that I am with you always."

God spoke to Farmer: "You have created a masterpiece. Do not hide your light under a bushel; persevere in accordance with your love of God."

Epilogue

And so it is done,
    I now count the cost:
no life have I had
    to save the soul lost.

For blessed from birth
    that was my mission,
to cast in God's waters
    and do some great fishin'.

So forget not God's love
    amidst your deep musing,
for indeed, Satan's head
    has received heavy bruising.

        – The Farmer

In the words of Jesus, "Let the hubbub begin."

www.bruisingtheheadofsatan.com